Pocket
SINGAPORE
TOP SIGHTS · LOCAL LIFE · MADE EASY

Ria de Jong, Cristian Bonetto

In This Book

QuickStart Guide

Your keys to understanding the city – we help you decide what to do and how to do it

Need to Know
Tips for a smooth trip

Neighbourhoods
What's where

Explore Singapore

The best things to see and do, neighbourhood by neighbourhood

Top Sights
Make the most of your visit

Local Life
The insider's city

The Best of Singapore

The city's highlights in handy lists to help you plan

Best Walks
See the city on foot

Singapore's Best...
The best experiences

Survival Guide

Tips and tricks for a seamless, hassle-free city experience

Getting Around
Travel like a local

Essential Information
Including where to stay

Our selection of the city's best places to eat, drink and experience:

◎ **Sights**

❌ **Eating**

🍺 **Drinking**

⭐ **Entertainment**

🔒 **Shopping**

These symbols give you the vital information for each listing:

☎ Telephone Numbers	♿ Family-Friendly
⊙ Opening Hours	🐾 Pet-Friendly
P Parking	🚌 Bus
⊖ Nonsmoking	⛴ Ferry
@ Internet Access	M MRT
⊚ Wi-Fi Access	S Subway
🌱 Vegetarian Selection	🚃 Tram
📖 English-Language Menu	🚆 Train

Find each listing quickly on maps for each neighbourhood:

Bar Hemingway

16 🍺 Map p233, B2

Legend has it that Hemi
self, wielding a machine
rate this timber-pan
ered bar during
showpiece is a
en by Papa ar
town. Dress
s.com; Hôtel Rit
; ⊙6.30pm-2a

Lonely Planet's Singapore

Lonely Planet Pocket Guides are designed to get you straight to the heart of the city.

Inside you'll find all the must-see sights, plus tips to make your visit to each one really memorable. We've split the city into easy-to-navigate neighbourhoods and provided clear maps so you'll find your way around with ease. Our expert authors have searched out the best of the city: walks, food, nightlife and shopping, to name a few. Because you want to explore, our 'Local Life' pages will take you to some of the most exciting areas to experience the real Singapore.

And of course you'll find all the practical tips you need for a smooth trip: itineraries for short visits, how to get around, and how much to tip the guy who serves you a drink at the end of a long day's exploration.

It's your guarantee of a really great experience.

Our Promise

You can trust our travel information because Lonely Planet authors visit the places we write about, each and every edition. We never accept freebies for positive coverage, so you can rely on us to tell it like it is.

QuickStart Guide 7

Explore Singapore 21

Worth a Trip:

QuickStart Guide

Welcome to Singapore

Smart, sharp and just a little sexy, Singapore is Southeast Asia's unexpected 'It kid', subverting staid stereotypes with ambitious architecture, dynamic museums, celebrity chefs and hip boutiques. Spike it with smoky temples, gut-rumble-inducing food markets and pockets of steamy jungle, and you'll find that Asia's former wallflower is a much more intriguing bloom than you ever gave it credit for.

Marina Bay
WSBOON IMAGES/GETTY IMAGES ©

Singapore
Top Sights

Gardens by the Bay (p26)

Singapore's most astounding green asset is a S$1 billion 'super park' that makes horticulture hot. Explore its futuristic bio-domes and Supertrees, traverse its panoramic Skyway, and keep an eye out for Marc Quinn's floating infant.

WSBOON IMAGES/GETTY IMAGES ©

National Gallery Singapore (p24)

Costing S$530 million and taking a decade to complete, this imposing complex is the jewel in Singapore's cultural crown. Its 8000-plus works constitute the world's largest collection of modern art from Singapore and Southeast Asia.

Singapore Botanic Gardens (p130)

Singapore's Garden of Eden is the perfect antidote to the city's rat-race tendencies. Obscenely lush and verdant, its 74 hectares are home to rare orchids, a swan-studded lake and a sultry, ginger-centric restaurant.

National Museum of Singapore (p28)

Evocative, interactive exhibitions and striking old-meets-new architecture underscore this showcase history museum. If you're after a gripping crash course in Singapore's backstory and culture, put this on your hit list.

Singapore Zoo (p125)

Singapore Zoo is one of the world's most inviting, enlightened animal sanctuaries, and a family-friendly must. Breakfast with orang-utans, sneak up to sleepy sloths and purr over rare white tigers.

Southern Ridges (p142)

Monkey-peppered jungle, sculptural forest walkways and arresting views over city and sea – the multipark Southern Ridges trail offers one of Singapore's most beautiful and accessible natural getaways.

Night Safari (p126)

Get up close and personal with a different kind of nightlife at this award-winning wildlife park, filled with an intriguing cast of free-roaming and free-flying creatures, great and small.

Chinatown Heritage Centre (p66)

Immerse yourself in the struggles, scandals and hard-core grit of Chinatown's roller-coaster past at this revamped museum. You'll find it on a lantern-festooned street once better known for opium dens and coolie traders.

Universal Studios (p116)

Home to the planet's tallest duelling roller coasters, Universal Studios cranks up the adrenalin with seven themed areas pimped with enough rides, razzle-dazzle spectaculars and movie-set kitsch to thrill the most hardened of inner children.

Singapore Local Life

Insider tips to help you find the real city

Once you've checked off the major sights, dig a little deeper and discover a more intimate side to the city – the side the locals know.

Chinatown Tastebuds & Temples (p68)
▶ Authentic hawker centres
▶ Hotspot bars and restaurants
The opium dens may have gone, but Chinatown's stubborn spirit kicks on with its in-yer-face market stalls, congee-slurping uncles and dragon-littered temples. Whether plonked on a plastic *kopitiam* (coffeeshop) stool or offering incense to the divine, prepare to savour enticing Chinatown.

Tiong Bahru (p62)
▶ Hip shops and cafes
▶ Heritage architecture
Not only famous for its art deco and mid-

20th-century domestic architecture, this low-rise, chilled-out neighbourhood draws the trendsetters and hipsters with its booty of clued-in cafes, trendy bars and restaurants, and quirky shops, not to mention its top-notch bookstores.

A Stroll in Little India (p94)
▶ Mosques and temples
▶ Street life
A riot of colours, scents and evening crowds, Little India bursts with pungent pavement stalls, authentic Indian grub and sari-peddling shops blaring Indian pop. Hunt down market spices, pimp your skin with henna, and feast your eyes on a whimsical, fairy-tale mosque.

Katong (p86)
▶ Peranakan heritage
▶ Restaurants
Multicoloured heritage shophouses, restaurant-filled streets and shops selling traditional ceramics, shoes and textiles. Katong is the heart and soul of Singapore's Peranakan culture. At its southern end is cycle-friendly East Coast Park, dotted with seafood eateries and bars facing a boat-laden sea.

Geylang (p88)
▶ Street food
▶ Nightlife
Gateway between heaven and hell, Geylang is as famed for its temples and mosques as it is for its *lorong* (alley) brothels, girly bars and cheap hotel rooms. Slip in at

Changi Beach

Lord Ganesh shrine in Little India

night for brilliant street food, karaoke and a rush that's more 'cheeky Bangkok' than 'strait-laced Singapore'.

Changi & Pulau Ubin (p90)

▶ Laid-back living
▶ Changi Museum & Chapel

Laid-back Changi peddles batik fabrics, Indian textiles and harrowing stories of Singapore under Japanese occupation at the moving Changi Museum & Chapel. Across the water, bicycle-friendly Pulau Ubin island channels a long-forgotten Singapore of ramshackle huts, old plantations and jungle-fringed country lanes.

KEVIN CLOGSTOUN/GETTY IMAGES ©

Other great places to experience the city like a local:

Chinatown Complex (p76)

Nylon Coffee Roasters (p75)

Colbar (p150)

Haji Lane (p113)

Jalan Besar (p107)

Gillman Barracks (p147)

Sri Veeramakaliamman Temple (p98)

Singapore Turf Club (p150)

Mustafa Centre (p113)

Rex Cinemas (p109)

Singapore
Day Planner

Day One

Start your Singapore fling with *kaya* (coconut jam) toast, runny eggs and strong *kopi* (coffee) at **Ya Kun Kaya Toast** (p78) before taking a riverside stroll at the **Quays** for a jaw-dropping urban panorama. Keep walking to the **National Museum of Singapore** (p28) or newer **National Gallery Singapore** (p24) for cultural insight, then feast on Peranakan dishes at **National Kitchen by Violet Oon** (p36).

Continue to Chinatown to soak up the sounds and scents of **Sri Mariamman Temple** (p72) and nearby **Buddha Tooth Relic Temple** (p72). For a rundown of the area's history, pop into the **Chinatown Heritage Centre** (p66). Alternatively, head up **Pinnacle@Duxton** (p74) for a bird's-eye view of the skyline and beyond, or de-stress with cheap reflexology at **People's Park Complex** (p74).

Opt for an early dinner at **Momma Kong's** (p74), **Ding Dong** (p75) or **Burnt Ends** (p74) before catching a taxi to the atmospheric **Night Safari** (p127). Alternatively, dine later and cap the night with well-mixed drinks at basement **Operation Dagger** (p78) or rooftop **Potato Head Folk** (p78).

Day Two

Little India will erase every preconceived notion of Singapore as a sterile, OCD metropolis. Weathered tailors stitch and sew by the side of the road, and the air is thick with cumin and Bollywood soundtracks. Take in the colours and chanting of **Sri Veeramakaliamman Temple** (p98) and buy a sari at **Tekka Centre** (p103). Learn more about the area's fascinating backstory at the new **Indian Heritage Centre** (p98), then choose-your-own-spice-level adventure at **Lagnaa Barefoot Dining** (p103).

Escape the afternoon heat in the air-conditioned comfort of **Orchard Road**. Purchase rare Singaporean prints and books at **Antiques of the Orient** (p59) and cognoscenti threads at **Robinsons** (p61) and **Sects Shop** (p59). Shopped out, it's time for happy-hour martinis at **Bar on 5** (p58) or beers on heritage beauty **Emerald Hill Road**.

If you're dining at **Satay by the Bay** (p38), you're already at **Gardens by the Bay** (p26). Give yourself plenty of time to explore Singapore's incredible new botanic gardens, including the Flower Dome and Cloud Forest conservatories. The gardens' Supertrees are especially spectacular during the nightly light show (7.45pm and 8.45pm).

Short on time?
We've arranged Singapore's must-sees into these day-by-day itineraries to make sure you see the very best of the city in the time you have available.

Day Three

☀ Wake up early to join the orang-utans for **Jungle Breakfast with Wildlife** (p125) at the world-class **Singapore Zoo**. There's lots of ground to cover so jump on the guided tram to get the lay of the land. Note feeding times as the animals are more active and you have the opportunity to get up-close and personal.

☀ After a quick lunch at the zoo, indulge in a little unadulterated fun on Singapore's pleasure island, **Sentosa**. Tackle rides both heart-racing and sedate at movie theme park **Universal Studios** (p116), or eye-up creatures great and small at the spectacular **SEA Aquarium** (p119). Alternatively, ride some artificial waves at **Wave House** (p120) or book an indoor skydive at **iFly** (p119).

☾ Slow down the pace with evening drinks on a palm-fringed Sentosa beach. Options include **Coastes** (p123) or the more secluded **Tanjong Beach Club** (p122). Come dinner, dine marina-side at **Mykonos on the Bay** (p122) or crank up the romance at **Il Lido at the Cliff** (p121). If you're travelling with kids, consider catching **Wings of Time** (p123), a multimillion-dollar sound, light and laser extravaganza.

Day Four

☀ For a taste of 1950s Singapore, head to Changi to catch a bumboat across to **Pulau Ubin**. Rent a bicycle and cycle the island's peaceful, jungle-fringed roads, passing tin-shacked houses, quirky shrines, and walking along a mangrove boardwalk. There's even a mountain-bike park with trails for varying skill levels.

☀ Once you've finished exploring sleepy **Pulau Ubin**, catch a bumboat back to Singapore. If it's not too late, pay a visit to the moving **Changi Museum & Chapel** (p91), which recounts the suffering and resilience of those who endured Singapore's Japanese occupation. If it is too late, wander the shops at **Changi Village**, stopping for a beer at **Coastal Settlement** (p91).

☾ Come evening, swap tranquil nostalgia for neon-lit excess in **Geylang**, a red-light district juxtaposed against temples, mosques and some of the best food in Singapore. Head back into town and end the night at trendy rooftop bar **Smoke and Mirrors** (p41), atop the **National Gallery Singapore**, where you can enjoy commanding views of the Marina Bay Sands spectacular nightly light-and-laser show.

Need to Know

For more information, see Survival Guide (p177)

Currency
Singapore dollar (S$)

Languages
English, Mandarin, Malay and Tamil

Visas
Citizens of the USA, UK, Australia, New Zealand, South Africa, most European countries and Asean nations (except Myanmar) do not require visas for stays of either 30 or 90 days, depending on the individual country. Other visitors may require visas. See www.ica.gov.sg for specifics.

Money
ATMs are widely available and credit cards are accepted in all hotels and most restaurants.

Mobile Phones
Singapore's two cell networks (GSM900 and GSM1800) are compatible with most of the world. Buy a local SIM card to keep costs down.

Time
Singapore Standard Time (GMT/UTC plus eight hours)

Plugs & Adaptors
Square, three-pin plugs of the type used in the UK; current is 220V to 240V.

Tipping
Largely unexpected and unnecessary.

① Before You Go

Your Daily Budget

Budget under S$200
▶ Dorm bed: S$20–40
▶ Meal at hawker centre: around S$6
▶ Ticket to a major museum: S$6–20

Midrange S$200–$350
▶ Double room in midrange hotel: S$140–250
▶ Two-course dinner with wine: S$70
▶ Cocktails at top bar: S$18–25 per drink

Top end over S$350
▶ Four- and five-star double room: S$250–700
▶ Top restaurant degustation: S$250 or more

Useful Websites

Lonely Planet (www.lonelyplanet.com/singapore) Destination low-down, hotel bookings.

Your Singapore (www.yoursingapore.com) Tourist site with handy planning feature.

Honeycombers (www.thehoneycombers.com) Covers events, eating, drinking and shopping.

Advance Planning

Two months before Book big-ticket events such as the Formula One race. Reserve a table at hot top-end restaurants.

One month before Book a bed if you are planning to stay in a dorm over the weekend.

One week before Look for last-minute deals on Singapore accommodation and check for any events or festivals. Book a posh hotel brunch.

2 Arriving in Singapore

Changi Airport (www.changiairport.com) is one of Asia's main air hubs and Singapore's major gateway.

▶ MRT trains run into town from the airport from 5.30am to midnight; public buses run from 6am to midnight. Both the train and bus trip cost from S$1.85.

▶ The airport shuttle bus (adult S$9, children S$6) runs 24 hours.

▶ A taxi into the city will cost anywhere from S$20 to S$40, and up to 50% more between midnight and 6am, plus airport surcharges.

▶ A four-seater limousine taxi costs S$55, plus S$15 surcharge per additional stop. Enquire at the ground transport desk at the airport.

✈ From Changi Airport

Destination	Best transport*
Colonial District, the Quays & Marina Bay	MRT
Orchard Rd	bus 36
Chinatown & the CBD	MRT
Little India & Kampong Glam	MRT
Sentosa	MRT, then Sentosa Express monorail
Holland Village, Dempsey Hill & the Botanic Gardens	Holland Village: MRT; Dempsey Hill: MRT, then bus 7, 75, 77, 105, 106, 123 or 174
West & Southwest Singapore	MRT

*Although more expensive, a taxi from Changi Airport is by far the quicker option, no matter which part of Singapore you're staying in.

3 Getting Around

Public transport is efficient, safe and relatively cheap.

Buy an EZ-Link card at MRT train station counters (S$12, including a S$5 nonrefundable deposit) to save time and money. Cards are valid on both trains and buses, as well as in many taxis.

Top up EZ-Link cards with cash or ATM cards at station ticket machines. The minimum top-up value is S$10.

MRT

Local metro with five colour-coded lines. Easiest way to get around. 5.30am–midnight.

Bus

Covers MRT areas and beyond. 6am–midnight, plus a handful of night services.

Taxi

Safe, honest and relatively cheap. Flag one at taxi stands or try your luck on the street. Book ahead if travelling in peak hours. Hefty surcharges apply during peak hours and from midnight to 6am.

Singapore Neighbourhoods

Worth a Trip

👁 **Top Sights**

Singapore Zoo (p124)

Night Safari (p126)

Holland Village, Dempsey Hill & the Botanic Gardens (p128)

Latte-sipping expats, boutique antiques in converted colonial barracks and the luxurious sprawl of Singapore Botanic Gardens. You've made it, lah!

👁 **Top Sights**

Singapore Botanic Gardens

Singapore Botanic Gardens 👁

West & Southwest Singapore (p140)

An urban getaway of jungle canopy walks, hilltop cocktails, historic war sites and an off-the-radar cultural gem.

👁 **Top Sights**

Southern Ridges

Southern Ridges 👁

Sentosa Island (p114)

Welcome to Fantasy Island, a 'think big' playground of theme parks, activities and shows, sunset beach bars and marina-side dining.

👁 **Top Sights**

Universal Studios

Universal Studios

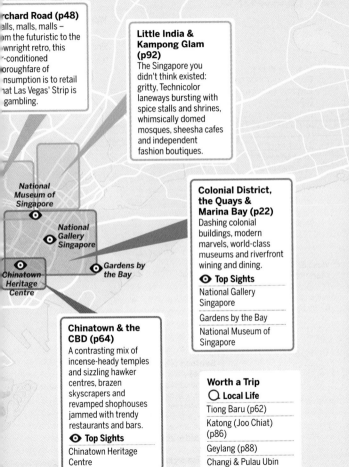

rchard Road (p48)
alls, malls, malls –
om the futuristic to the
wnright retro, this
r-conditioned
oroughfare of
nsumption is to retail
nat Las Vegas' Strip is
gambling.

Little India & Kampong Glam (p92)
The Singapore you didn't think existed: gritty, Technicolor laneways bursting with spice stalls and shrines, whimsically domed mosques, sheesha cafes and independent fashion boutiques.

National Museum of Singapore

National Gallery Singapore

Chinatown Heritage Centre

Gardens by the Bay

Colonial District, the Quays & Marina Bay (p22)
Dashing colonial buildings, modern marvels, world-class museums and riverfront wining and dining.

◉ Top Sights

National Gallery Singapore

Gardens by the Bay

National Museum of Singapore

Chinatown & the CBD (p64)
A contrasting mix of incense-heady temples and sizzling hawker centres, brazen skyscrapers and revamped shophouses jammed with trendy restaurants and bars.

◉ Top Sights

Chinatown Heritage Centre

Worth a Trip
◯ Local Life

Explore
Singapore

Worth a Trip

Marina Bay Sands Hotel & ArtScience Museum by night
/GETTY IMAGES ©

Explore

Colonial District, the Quays & Marina Bay

The Colonial District dazzles with its 19th-century buildings, A-list museums and sprawling malls. Just south, the sinuous Singapore River is where you'll find the Quays and their booty of restaurants, bars and clubs. East of here, the river spills into Marina Bay, home to botanical blockbuster Gardens by the Bay (pictured above) and resort, casino, and entertainment-and-dining complex Marina Bay Sands.

The Sights in a Day

Start the morning with a saunter along the Singapore River, taking in Singapore's dramatic skyline. Right beside the river is the **Asian Civilisations Museum** (p32), home to a breathtaking collection of artefacts from across Asia. Alternatively, explore the coveted collection of Southeast Asian art at **National Gallery Singapore** (p24).

If your belly is rumbling, the National Gallery Singapore has several dining options, including the highly acclaimed Peranakan restaurant **National Kitchen by Violet Oon** (p36). Belly full, culture vultures can continue their cultural enlightenment at the **National Museum of Singapore** (p28) or **Peranakan Museum** (p32). Alternatively, shop for local design at **Naiise** (p45) or mall trawl **Shoppes at Marina Bay Sands** (p47).

Come dinner, nosh hawker-style at **Satay by the Bay** (p38), located at the spectacular **Gardens by the Bay** (p26). Highlights here include the Flower Dome, Cloud Forest and bird's-eye OCBC Skyway. Stay for the sound-and-light show, Garden Rhapsody, then tie things up with a toast at **Lantern** (p42) or **Smoke and Mirrors** (p41).

◉ Top Sights

Gardens by the Bay (p26)

National Gallery Singapore (p24)

National Museum of Singapore (p28)

♥ Best of Singapore

Food

National Kitchen by Violet Oon (p36)

Odette (p36)

Gluttons Bay (p37)

Drinking

Smoke and Mirrors (p41)

Landing Point (p41)

Southbridge (p41)

Getting There

Ⓜ **MRT** City Hall (Red and Green Lines) and Dhoby Ghaut (Purple, Red and Yellow Lines) are the best MRT stops for the Colonial District. City Hall is connected via underground malls to Esplanade (Yellow Line). Raffles Place (Red and Green Lines) and Clarke Quay (Purple Line) serve the Quays. Marina Bay (Red Line) and Bayfront (Yellow and Blue Lines) service Marina Bay Sands.

Top Sights
National Gallery Singapore

Ten years in the making, the S$530 million National Gallery is a befitting home for what is one of the world's most important surveys of colonial and post-colonial Southeast Asian art. Housed in the historic City Hall and Old Supreme Court buildings, its 8000-plus collection of 19th-century and modern Southeast Asian art fills two major gallery spaces.

👁 Map p30, E3

www.nationalgallery.sg

St Andrew's Rd

adult/child S$20/15

🕙 10am-7pm Sun-Thu, to 10pm Fri & Sat

Ⓜ City Hall

Don't Miss

The Buildings

Unified by a striking aluminium and glass canopy, Singapore's former City Hall and Old Supreme Court buildings are now joined to create the country's largest visual arts venue at 64,000 sq metres. Enter via the St Andrew's Rd door to get a real appreciation of how these two colonial giants have been seamlessly connected. Tours are held twice daily; don't miss the court holding cells, where many of Singapore's accused waited to hear their fates.

DBS Singapore Gallery

Titled 'Siapa Nama Kamu?' (Malay for 'what is your name?'), this gallery showcases a comprehensive overview of Singaporean art from the 19th century to today. Don't miss the *Portrait of Lee Boon Ngan* in Gallery Two; take note of how her collar sparkles. Also in this gallery, look out for the black-and-white woodblock prints; *Seascape* was a collaboration of six artists. Finally, have your mind bent by *Chair,* remade especially for the gallery.

UOB Southeast Asia Gallery

Examining the art and artistic contexts of the greater Southeast Asia region, this gallery is housed in the Old Supreme Court. Step into the darkened Gallery One, once a courtroom and now filled with art and pieces from the second half of the 19th century when most of Southeast Asia was under colonial rule. Be confronted in Gallery Three by Raden Saleh's wall-filling *Forest Fire;* however, it's the *Wounded Lion,* also by Raden Saleh, that may give you a fright. Also noteworthy are the brightly coloured Vietnamese propaganda posters in Gallery 11.

☑ Top Tip

▶ The museum runs free one-hour tours through the galleries and also of the buildings' highlights. Only 20 slots are available on a first come, first served basis. Registration opens 20 minutes before each tour at the Tour Desk, B1 Concourse. Check the website for start times.

✖ Take a Break

If you need a little pit stop or some retail therapy, head to **Gallery & Co.** (☏6385 6683; www.galleryand.co; 01-05 & 01-17 City Hall Wing, National Gallery Singapore; ⏰10am-7pm Mon-Thu, to 10pm Fri-Sun) on level 1. Here you'll find designer books, accessories and souvenirs.

There are two food outlets in the museum; however, the coffee and cupcakes served near the Keppel Centre entrance are the best.

Top Sights
Gardens by the Bay

Welcome to the botanic gardens of the future, a fantasy land of space-age bio-domes, high-tech Supertrees and whimsical sculptures. Costing S$1 billion and sprawling across 101 hectares of reclaimed land, Gardens by the Bay is more than just a mind-clearing patch of green. This ambitious masterpiece of urban planning is as thrilling to architecture buffs as it is to nature lovers.

Map p30, H5

6420 6848

www.gardensbythebay.com.sg

18 Marina Gardens Dr

gardens free, conservatories adult/child S$28/15

5am-2am, conservatories

Bayfront

Cloud Forest Dome

Don't Miss

The Conservatories

Housing 217,000 plants from 800 species, the Gardens' asymmetrical conservatories rise like giant paper nautilus shells beside Marina Bay. The **Flower Dome** replicates a dry, Mediterranean climate and includes ancient olive trees. It's also home to sophisticated restaurant **Pollen**, which sources ingredients from the gardens. **Cloud Forest Dome's** a steamy affair, recreating the tropical montane climate found at elevations between 1500m and 3000m. Its centrepiece is a 35m-high mountain complete with waterfall.

Supertrees & Sculptures

Sci-fi meets botany at the Supertrees, 18 steel-clad concrete structures adorned with over 162,900 plants. Actually massive exhausts for the Gardens' bio-mass steam turbines, they're used to generate electricity to cool the conservatories. For a sweeping view, walk across the 22m-high **OCBC Skyway** (⏱ 9am-9pm), connecting six Supertrees at Supertree Grove, where tickets (S$8, cash only) are purchased. Each night at 7.45pm and 8.45pm, the Supertrees become the glowing protagonists of Garden Rhapsody, a light-and-sound spectacular.

The most visually arresting of the Gardens' numerous artworks is Mark Quinn's colossal *Planet*. Created in 2008 and donated to Gardens by the Bay, the sculpture is a giant seven-month-old infant, fast asleep and seemingly floating above the ground. This illusion is nothing short of brilliant, especially considering the bronze bubba comes in at a hefty 7 tonnes. The work was modelled on Quinn's own son.

☑ **Top Tips**

▶ The best time to visit is late afternoon or early evening, when the heat softens and the Supertrees become the protagonists of the mesmerising sound-and-light show Garden Rhapsody, nightly at 7.45pm and 8.45pm.

▶ Gardens by the Bay operates a handy, on-site shuttle bus. Purchase tickets on board (small denominations of cash only). Note that services begin at 12.30pm on the first Monday of the month.

✖ **Take a Break**

Fine dine in the Flower Dome at Pollen (p37). The restaurant also hosts an excellent afternoon tea.

For a cheaper feed, opt for alfresco hawker centre Satay by the Bay (p38).

Top Sights
National Museum of Singapore

Imaginative, prodigiously stocked and brilliantly designed, Singapore's National Museum is good enough to warrant two visits. Recently revamped, the space ditches staid exhibits for lively multi-media galleries that bring Singapore's jam-packed biography to vivid life. It's an intimate, intriguing journey, spanning ancient Malay royalty and colonial-era backstabbing to 20th-century rioting, reinvention, food, fashion and film.

Map p30, D1

6332 3659

www.nationalmuseum.sg

93 Stamford Rd

adult/child, student & senior S$10/5

10am-6.30pm

Dhoby Ghaut, Bras Basah

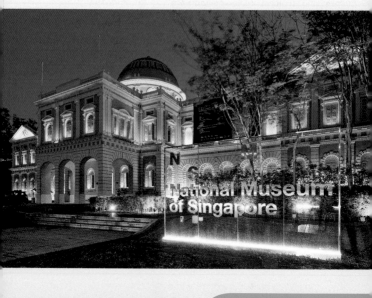

Don't Miss

History Gallery

Spanning six centuries, the History Gallery will have you peering into opium dens, confronting harrowing tales of Japanese occupation and even smelling the stench of the old Singapore River! On level two, exhibitions magically recreate snapshots of everyday life in Singapore over the past 100 years – from the buzz and fashion of the colonial era, to stories of resilience and hope from war survivors. It's rounded off with the emergence of Singapore as a nation through arts and culture. The final exhibition, Desire and Danger, showcases exquisite 19th-century botanical watercolours commissioned by Singapore's first resident and commandant, William Farquhar. Adding further layers of enlightenment are the museum's top-notch temporary exhibitions, which cover subjects as diverse as post-independence art to the history of Singapore motor racing.

Art Installations & Architecture

The museum features several striking indoor and outdoor art installations, among them *Pedas Pedas,* a giant bronze chilli on the lawn at the back of the complex. Created for the museum by Singapore-based conceptual artist Kumari Nahappan, the chilli can be seen as a metaphor for Singapore: small and hot, yet powerful and energetic.

Last but not least is the museum's outstanding architecture. The superb neoclassical wing, built in 1887 as the Raffles Library and Museum, boasts a breathtaking rotunda, lavished with 50 panels of stained glass. A sleek extension features a Glass Passage, with revealing views of the dome's exterior, as well as its own dramatic, 16m-high Glass Rotunda.

☑ Top Tips

▶ If you're a history buff make sure to set aside about four hours to cover the museum. Once you've finished, exit from the top level and enjoy a wander around Fort Canning Park, where some of Singapore's historic events took place.

▶ Free guided tours are offered daily; check the website for times.

▶ Entry is free to the Living Galleries from 6pm to 8pm daily.

✕ Take a Break

If you need to rest your tired feet head to **Food for Thought** (📞6338 9887; www.foodforthought. com.sg; 01-04/05, National Museum of Singapore; mains S$16-25; ⏱10am-6.30pm Sun-Thu, 10am-9pm Fri & Sat) for a quick meal, or coffee and cake.

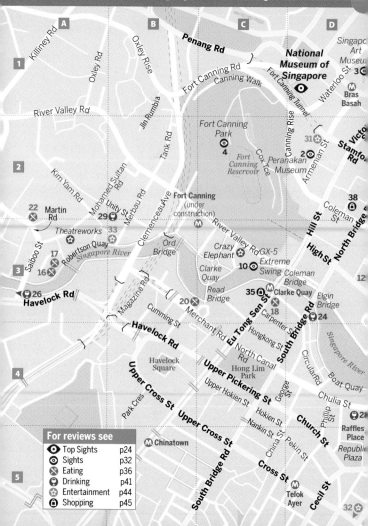

For reviews see

◉	Top Sights	p24
◉	Sights	p32
⊗	Eating	p36
🍷	Drinking	p41
★	Entertainment	p44
🔒	Shopping	p45

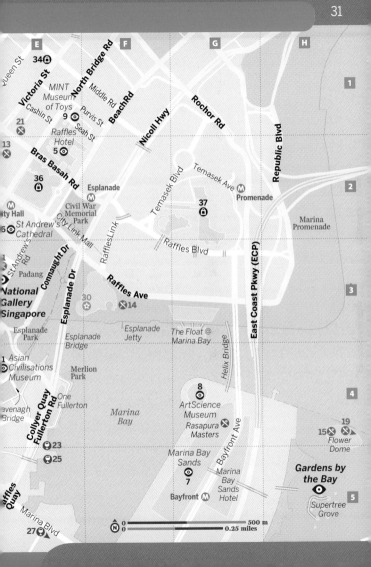

E
34

Queen St
Victoria St
North Bridge Rd
F
Middle Rd
Beach Rd
Nicoll Hwy
Rochor Rd
G
H
1

MINT
Museum
of Toys
Cashin St
21
13
Bras Basah Rd
Purvis St
Seah St
9
Raffles
Hotel
5

Republic Blvd

2

36

Esplanade

Civil War
Memorial
Park
ity Hall
St Andrew's
Cathedral
St Andrew's Rd
Padang
Connaught Dr
RafflesLink
City Link Mall
Temasek Blvd
Temasek Ave
37
Promenade

Temasek Blvd
Raffles Blvd

Marina
Promenade

2

National
Gallery
Singapore
30
Esplanade Dr
Raffles Ave
14
East Coast Pkwy (ECP)

3

Esplanade
Park
Esplanade
Bridge
Esplanade
Jetty
The Float @
Marina Bay
Helix Bridge

Asian
Civilisations
Museum
avenagh
Bridge
Merlion
Park
One Fullerton
Marina
Bay
8
ArtScience
Museum
Rasapura
Masters

4

Collyer Quay
Fullerton Rd
23
25
Marina Bay
Sands
7
Bayfront
Bayfront Ave
Marina
Bay
Sands
Hotel
19
15
Flower
Dome

Gardens by
the Bay

affles
Quay
Marina Blvd
27

N 0   500 m
0   0.25 miles

Supertree
Grove

5

Sights

Asian Civilisations Museum
MUSEUM

1 ◉ Map p30, E4

This remarkable museum houses the region's most comprehensive collection of pan-Asian treasures. Its galleries explore the history, cultures and religions of Southeast Asia, China, the Asian subcontinent and Islamic West Asia. Currently undergoing a radical transformation, including two additional wings, the new galleries will be curated to emphasise the cross-cultural connections developed due to Singapore's history as a port city. Already open, the Tang Shipwreck showcases over 500 pieces of recovered booty. All galleries will be open in 2017. (☑6332 7798; www.acm.org.sg; 1 Empress Pl; adult/child under 6yr S$8/free, 7-9pm Fri half-price; ☉10am-7pm Sat-Thu, to 9pm Fri; Ⓜ Raffles Place)

Peranakan Museum
MUSEUM

2 ◉ Map p30, D2

This is the best spot to explore the rich heritage of the Peranakans (Straits Chinese descendants). Thematic galleries cover various aspects of Peranakan culture, from the traditional 12-day wedding ceremony to crafts, spirituality and feasting. Look out for intricately detailed ceremonial costumes and beadwork, beautifully carved wedding beds, and rare dining porcelain. An especially curious example of Peranakan fusion culture is a pair of Victorian bell jars in which statues of Christ and the Madonna are adorned with Chinese-style flowers and vines. (☑6332 7591; www.peranakanmuseum.org.sg; 39 Armenian St; adult/child under 7yr S$6/free, 7-9pm Fri half-price; ☉10am-7pm, to 9pm Fri; Ⓜ City Hall)

Singapore Art Museum
MUSEUM

3 ◉ Map p30, D1

Formerly the St Joseph's Institution – a Catholic boys' school – SAM now sings the praises of contemporary Southeast Asian art. Themed exhibitions include works from the museum's permanent collection as well as those from private collections, from painting and sculpture to video art and site-specific installations. Free, 45-minute guided tours of the museum are conducted in English two to three times daily; check the website for times. (SAM; ☑6589 9580; www.singaporeartmuseum.sg; 71 Bras Basah Rd; adult/student & senior S$10/5, 6-9pm Fri free; ☉10am-7pm Sat-Thu, to 9pm Fri; Ⓜ Bras Basah)

Fort Canning Park
PARK

4 ◉ Map p30, C2

When Raffles rolled into Singapore, locals steered clear of Fort Canning Hill, then called Bukit Larangan (Forbidden Hill) out of respect for the sacred shrine of Sultan Iskandar Shah, ancient Singapura's last ruler. These

Asian Civilisations Museum

days, the hill is better known as Fort Canning Park, a lush retreat from the hot streets below. Amble through the spice garden, catch an exhibition at **Singapore Pinacothéque de Paris** (✆6883 1588; www.pinacotheque.com.sg; 5 Cox Tce; Heritage Gallery, Graffiti Walk & Garden Walk free, all galleries adult/student/child under 7yr S\$28/19/9; ⏱10am-6pm; Ⓜ Dhoby Ghaut) or ponder Singapore's wartime defeat at the **Battlebox Museum** (✆6338 6133; www.battlebox.com.sg; 2 Cox Tce; adult/child S\$18/9; ⏱tours 1.30pm, 2.45pm & 4pm Mon, 9.45am, 11am, 1.30pm, 2.45pm & 4pm Tue-Sun; Ⓜ Dhoby Ghaut). (www.nparks.gov.sg; bounded by Hill St, Canning Rise, Clemenceau Ave & River Valley Rd; Ⓜ Dhoby Ghaut, Clarke Quay)

Raffles Hotel
NOTABLE BUILDING

5 ◉ Map p30, E2

Although its resplendent lobby is only accessible to hotel guests and its bars are little more than tourist traps, Singapore's most iconic slumber palace is worth a quick visit for its magnificent ivory frontage, famous Sikh doorman and lush, hushed tropical grounds. The hotel started life in 1887 as a modest 10-room bungalow fronting the beach (long gone thanks to land reclamation), and it still evokes the days when Singapore was a swampy, tiger-tempered outpost of the British Empire. (✆6337 1886; www.raffleshotel.com; 1 Beach Rd; Ⓜ City Hall)

Local Life
Burmese Peninsula

Hop off at City Hall MRT station, cross North Bridge Rd, and you might just think you've hit a vertical Yangon. In truth you're in **Peninsula Plaza** (Map p30, D3; www.peninsulaplaza.com.sg; 111 North Bridge Rd; ⏰9am-9pm; **M**City Hall) mall, Singapore's unofficial 'Little Burma'. Among the moneychangers, camera shops and sprawling Bata shoe shop is a legion of Burmese businesses, from visa and travel agencies to cluttered tailors and minimarts, stalls selling sweet Burmese tea, and even betel nut stands peddling folded leaves of the mild stimulant. For a mouth-watering Burmese feed, head to basement **Inle Myanmar** (☎6333 5438; www.inlemyanmar.com.sg; B1-07 (A/B), North Bridge Rd; dishes S$8-25; ⏰11am-10pm Mon-Sat, from 10am Sun; 🛜; **M**City Hall).

St Andrew's Cathedral   CHURCH

6 ◎ Map p30, E2

Funded by Scottish merchants and built by Indian convicts, this wedding cake of a cathedral stands in stark contrast to the glass and steel surrounding it. Completed in 1838 but torn down and rebuilt in its present form in 1862 after lightning damage, it's one of Singapore's finest surviving examples of English Gothic architecture. Interesting details include the tropics-friendly *porte-cochère* (carriage porch) entrance – designed to shelter passengers – and the colourful stained glass adorning the western wall. (☎6337 6104; www.livingstreams.org.sg; 11 St Andrew's Rd; ⏰9am-5pm; **M**City Hall)

Marina Bay Sands   COMPLEX

7 ◎ Map p30, G5

Designed by Israeli-born architect Moshe Safdie, Marina Bay Sands is a sprawling hotel, casino, mall, theatre, exhibition and museum complex. Star of the show is the **Marina Bay Sands** hotel, (☎6688 8888; www.marinabay-sands.com; 10 Bayfront Ave; r from S$500; ❄@🛜🏊; **M**Bayfront) its three 55-storey towers connected by a cantilevered SkyPark. Head up for a drink and stellar views at **CÉ LA VI** (☎6688 7688; www.sg.celavi.com; Level 57, ⏰noon-late), the sky bar formerly known as Ku De Ta. Each night, the complex dazzles with its 15-minute light-and-laser spectacular, Wonder Full. (www.marinabaysands.com; Marina Bay; **M**Bayfront)

ArtScience Museum   MUSEUM

8 ◎ Map p30, G4

Designed by prolific Moshe Safdie and looking like a giant white lotus, the lily pond–framed ArtScience Museum hosts major international travelling exhibitions in fields as varied as art, design, media, science and technology. Expect anything from explorations of deep-sea creatures to retrospectives of world-famous industrial designers. (☎6688 8826; www.marinabaysands.com/museum; Marina Bay Sands; average prices adult/child under 13yr S$17/9; ⏰10am-7pm, last admission 6pm; **M**Bayfront)

MINT Museum of Toys   MUSEUM

9 ◉ Map p30, E1

Nostalgia rules at this slinky ode to playtime, its four skinny floors home to over 50,000 vintage toys. You'll see everything from rare Flash Gordon comics and supersonic toy guns to original Mickey Mouse dolls and oh-so-wrong golliwogs from 1930s Japan. Stock up on whimsical toys at the lobby shop or celebrate adulthood with a stiff drink at the adjacent **Mr Punch Rooftop Bar** (☎6339 6266; www.mrpunch.com; 26 Seah St; ☺3-11.30pm Mon-Thu, to 2am Fri, 11am-11.30pm Sat, to 6pm Sun; Ⓜ City Hall, Esplanade). (☎6339 0660; www.emint.com; 26 Seah St; adult/child S$15/7.50; ☺9.30am-6.30pm; Ⓜ City Hall, Esplanade)

GX-5 Extreme Swing   ADVENTURE SPORTS

10 ◉ Map p30, C3

A relatively gentle high ('relatively' is the key here) is offered right next door to the **G-Max Bungy** (☎6338 1766; www.gmax.com.sg; 3E River Valley Rd; adult/student per ride S$45/35, incl GX-5 Extreme Swing S$69/50; ☺2pm-late; Ⓜ Clarke Quay). Whereas the G-Max offers a

Understand

Singlish, lah!

While there isn't a Singlish grammar as such, there are definite characteristics. Verb tenses tend to be nonexistent. Past, present and future are indicated instead by time indicators, so in Singlish it's 'I go tomorrow' or 'I go yesterday'. Long stress is placed on the last syllable of phrases, so that the standard English 'government' becomes 'guvva-*men*'.

Words ending in consonants are often syncopated and vowels are often distorted. A Chinese-speaking taxi driver might not immediately understand that you want to go to Perak Rd, since they know it as 'Pera Roh'.

A typical exchange might – confusingly – go something like this: 'Eh, this Sunday you going cheong (party) anot? No ah? Why like that? Don't be so boring lah!' Prepositions and pronouns are dropped, word order is flipped, phrases are clipped short, and stress and cadence are unconventional, to say the least.

The particle 'lah' is often tagged on to the end of sentences for emphasis, as in 'No good lah'. Requests or questions may be marked with a tag ending, since direct questioning can be rude. As a result, questions that are formed to be more polite often come across to Westerners as rude. 'Would you like a beer?' becomes 'You wan beer or not?'

For more, check out the Coxford Singlish Dictionary on the satirical website Talking Cock (www.talkingcock.com).

straight-up face-peeling vertical trip, the GX-5 swings riders up and over the Singapore River with somewhat less nauseating velocity. (✆6338 1766; www.gmax.com.sg; 3E River Valley Rd; adult/ reduced per ride S$45/35, incl G-Max Reverse Bungy S$69/50; ◷2pm-late; ⓂClarke Quay)

Eating

National Kitchen by Violet Oon
PERANAKAN $$

11 ✕ Map p30, E3

Chef Violet Oon is a national treasure, much loved for her faithful Peranakan (Chinese-Malay fusion) dishes – so much so that she was chosen to open her latest venture inside Singapore's showcase National Gallery (p24). Feast on made-from-scratch beauties like sweet, spicy *kueh pie teҫ* (prawn- and yam bean–stuffed pastry cups), dry laksa and fried turmeric chicken wings with chinchalok sambal. (✆9834 9935; www.violetoon.com; National Gallery Singapore, 1 St Andrew's Rd; dishes S$15-42; ◷noon-2.30pm & 6-9.30pm; ⓂCity Hall)

Odette
MODERN FRENCH $$$

12 ✕ Map p30, D3

Muscling in on Singapore's saturated fine dining scene, this modern French restaurant had people talking even before the first dish left the kitchen. With former **Jaan** (✆6837 3322; www.jaan.com.sg; 70th fl, Swissôtel The Stamford, 2 Stamford Rd; lunch/dinner set menus from S$78/168; ◷noon-2pm & 7-10pm Mon-Sat; ✕; ⓂCity Hall) chef Julien Royer at the helm, menus are guided by the seasons and expertly crafted. The space is visually stunning, with a soft colour palette and floating aerial installation by local artist Dawn Ng.

Book at least a month in advance. (✆6385 0498; www.odetterestaurant. com; 01-04, National Gallery, 1 St Andrew's Rd; lunch from S$88, dinner from S$208; ◷noon-1.30pm Tue-Sat, 7-9pm Mon-Sat; ✕; ⓂCity Hall)

Whitegrass
MODERN AUSTRALIAN $$$

13 ✕ Map p30, E2

It's all about the details in this fine dining establishment helmed by chef-owner Sam Aisbett. From the air-flown Australian produce, Roland Lannier steak knives and painted mural by local illustrator MessyMsxi (don't mistake it for wallpaper), everything is effortlessly chic. The menu has Japanese and Asian influences; a highlight is the Western Australian marron with desert lime, pickled and grilled cucumber, young garlic, breakfast radish and beach succulents. (✆6837 0402; www.whitegrass.com.sg; 01-26/27, Chijmes, 30 Victoria St; 2-/3-/5-course lunch S$48/64/135, 5-/8-course dinner S$170/265; ◷6.30-9.30pm Mon-Wed & Sat, noon-2.15pm & 6.30-9.30pm Thu & Fri; ✕; ⓂCity Hall, Bras Basah)

Diners at Gluttons Bay

Gluttons Bay

HAWKER $

14 Map p30, F3

Selected by the *Makansutra Food Guide,* this row of alfresco hawker stalls is a great place to start your Singapore food odyssey. Get indecisive over classics like oyster omelette, satay, barbecue stingray and carrot cake (opt for the black version). Its central, bayside location makes it a huge hit, so be sure to head in either early or late to avoid the frustrating hunt for a table. (www. makansutra.com; 01-15, Esplanade Mall, 8 Raffles Ave; dishes from S$5; ⏰5pm-2am Mon-Thu, to 3am Fri & Sat, 4pm-1am Sun; Ⓜ Esplanade)

Pollen

EUROPEAN $$$

15 Map p30, H4

Inside Gardens by the Bay's Flower Dome (free entry when dining), posh Pollen is the Singapore spin-off of London's lauded Pollen Street Social. Its menus deliver artful, produce-driven European flavours with subtle Asian inflections. The three-course set lunch (S$55) is good value, while Pollen's more casual upstairs cafe serves a fine afternoon high tea from 3pm to 5pm Wednesday to Monday (book at least a week ahead). (📞6604 9988; www.pollen. com.sg; Flower Dome, Gardens by the Bay, 18 Marina Gardens Dr; mains S$40-70, 5-course dinner tasting menu S$180; ⏰noon-2.30pm & 6-9.30pm Wed-Mon, Pollen Terrace cafe 9am-9pm; Ⓜ Bayfront)

Super Loco   MEXICAN $$

16 Map p30, A3

The only thing missing is a beach at this breezy hipster cantina, complete with Mexican party vibe, pink-neon and playful barkeeps in Cancún-esque shirts. Get the good times rolling with a competent frozen margarita, then lick your lips over the standout ceviche, zingy crab and avocado tostada, and the damn fine *pescado* (fish) tacos. (☎6235 8900; www.super-loco.com; 01-13, Robertson Quay; tacos S$8-12, quesadillas S$14-16; ◷5-10.30pm Mon-Thu, to 11pm Fri, 10am-3.30pm & 5-11pm Sat, to 10pm Sun; ▭51, 64, 123, 143, 186)

Curry Culture   INDIAN $$

17 Map p30, A3

Softly lit and semi-alfresco, this outstanding Indian restaurant offers flavour-packed, nuanced dishes like tangy *papdi chaat* (crisp dough wafers topped with spiced potato, yoghurt and chutney), seductive *Hyderabadi baingan* (eggplant in a fresh coconut and peanut sauce), and a spectacular *bhuna gosht* (spiced, slow-cooked lamb with caramelised onion). Cool things down with a soothing ginger lassi, made with fried curry leaf for added complexity. (☎6235 6134; www.thecurryculture.com.sg; 01-10/11, 60 Robertson Quay; mains S$14-28; ◷5-10.30pm Mon-Thu, 12.30-2pm & 5-10.30pm Fri-Sun; ▨; ▭51, 64, 123, 143, 186)

Song Fa Bak Kut Teh   CHINESE $

18 Map p30, C3

If you need a hug, this cult-status eatery delivers with its *bak kut teh*. Literally 'meat bone tea', it's a soothing concoction of fleshy pork ribs simmered in a peppery broth of herbs, spices and whole garlic cloves. The ribs are sublimely soft, sweet and melt-in-the-mouth, and staff will happily refill your bowl with broth. (☎6533 6128; www.songfa.com.sg; 11 New Bridge Rd; dishes S$6-11.50; ◷9am-9.15pm Tue-Sun; Ⓜ Clarke Quay)

Satay by the Bay   HAWKER $

19 Map p30, H4

Gardens by the Bay's own hawker centre has an enviable location, alongside Marina Bay and far from the roar of city traffic. Especially evocative at night, it's known for its satay, best devoured under open skies on the spacious wooden deck. As you'd expect, prices are a little higher than at more local hawker centres, with most dishes between S$8 and S$10. (www.gardensbythebay.com.sg; Gardens by the Bay, 18 Marina Gardens Dr; dishes from S$4; ◷food stalls vary, drinks stall 24hr; Ⓜ Bayfront)

Jumbo Seafood   CHINESE $$$

20 Map p30, B3

If you're lusting after chilli crab – and you should be – this is a good place to indulge. The gravy is sweet and nutty, with just the right amount of chilli. Make sure to order some *mantou* (fried buns) to soak up the gravy. While all of Jumbo's outlets have the dish down to an art, this one has the best riverside location. (📞6532 3435; www.jumboseafood.com.sg; 01-01/02 Riverside Point, 30 Merchant Rd; dishes from S$12, chilli crab around S$78 per kg; ⏱noon-2.15pm & 6-11.15pm; Ⓜ Clarke Quay)

Wah Lok
CHINESE $$

21 🍴 Map p30, E1

This plush Cantonese classic serves one of Singapore's best dim-sum lunches. There are no trolley-pushing aunties here, just a dedicated yum-cha menu and gracious staff ready to take your order (must-eats include the *xiaolongbao* soup dumplings, and baked barbecued-pork buns). There are two lunch sittings per day on weekends; book three days ahead to dine then. (📞6311 8188; www.carltonhotel.sg; Level 2, Carlton Hotel, 76 Bras Basah Rd; dim sum S$5-6.90, mains S$20-40; ⏱11.30am-2.15pm & 6.30-10.15pm Mon-Sat, 11am-2.15pm & 6.30-10.15pm Sun; 🛜; Ⓜ City Hall, Bras Basah)

Understand
Quays of the City

The stretch of riverfront that separates the Colonial District from the CBD is known as the Quays.

Boat Quay (Ⓜ Raffles Place, Clarke Quay) Boat Quay was once Singapore's centre of commerce, and remained an important economic area into the 1960s. The area became a major entertainment district in the 1990s, filled with touristy bars, shops and menu-clutching touts. Discerning punters ditch these for the growing number of clued-in cafes and drinking dens dotting the streets behind the main strip.

Clarke Quay (www.clarkequay.com.sg; Ⓜ Clarke Quay) How much time you spend in Clarke Quay really depends upon your personal taste in aesthetics. If pastel hues, Dr Seuss–style design, and lad-and-ladette hang-outs are your schtick, you'll be well in your element. Fans of understated cool, however, should steer well clear.

Robertson Quay (🚌54, 64, 123, 139, 143, 186, Ⓜ Clarke Quay) At the furthest reach of the river, Robertson Quay was once used for the storage of goods. Now some of the old *godown* have found new purposes as bars and members-only party places. The vibe here is more 'grown up' than Clarke Quay, attracting a 30-plus crowd generally more interested in wining, dining and conversation than getting hammered to Top 40 hits.

WSBOON IMAGES/GETTY IMAGES ©

Clark Quay (p39) by night

Common Man Coffee Roasters

CAFE $$

22  Map p30, A2

While this airy, industrial-cool cafe roasts and serves top-class coffee, it also serves seriously scrumptious grub. Produce is super fresh and the combinations simple yet inspired, from all-day brekkie winners like green-pea fritters with crispy pancetta and balsamic syrup, to a lunchtime quinoa salad with grilled sweet potato, spinach, mint, coriander, goat's cheese and honey-raisin yoghurt. (📞6836 4695; www.commonmancoffeeroasters.com; 22 Martin Rd; mains S$19-29; ⏰7.30am-5.30pm; 🛜🍴; 🚌32, 54, 64, 123, 139, 143, 195)

Pizzeria Mozza

ITALIAN $$

This dough-kneading favourite (see 7 ⊚ Map p30, G5) is co-owned by prolific New York chef Mario Batali. While it's hardly a bargain, it is one of the few celeb-chef eateries at Marina Bay Sands (p34) that won't have you remortgaging the house. While both the antipasti and panini should appease the pickiest nonnas, the stars are the wood-fired pizzas, with crispy crusts to die for. (📞6688 8522; www.singapore.pizzeriamozza.com; B1-42/46, The Shoppes at Marina Bay Sands, 2 Bayfront Ave; pizzas S$20-38; ⏰noon-10.45pm; Ⓜ️Bayfront)

Drinking

Smoke and Mirrors BAR

We're calling it: this chic new bar (see 11 ⊗ Map p30, E3) offers the best view of Singapore. Perched on the top of the National Gallery (p24), Smoke and Mirrors looks out over the Padang to Marina Bay Sands and is flanked by skyscrapers on either side. Arrive before sunset so you can sit, drink in hand, and watch the city transition from day to night. Book ahead and request front-row seats. (📞9234 8122; www.smokeandmirrors.com.sg; 06-01, National Gallery Singapore, 1 St Andrew's Rd; ⏰noon-midnight Sun-Thu, to 2am Fri & Sat; Ⓜ City Hall)

Landing Point LOUNGE

23 🚇 Map p30, E4

For a decadent high tea, it's hard to beat the one at this chichi waterside lounge. Book ahead (one day for weekdays, two weeks for weekends), style up, and head in on an empty stomach. Steaming pots of TWG tea are paired with drool-inducing morsels like truffled-egg sandwiches, melt-in-your-mouth quiche, brioche buns topped with duck and blueberries, and caramel-filled dark-chocolate tarts. (📞6597 5277; www.fullertonbayhotel.com; Fullerton Bay Hotel, 80 Collyer Quay; high tea per adult S$45, with glass of champagne S$65, per child S$22; ⏰9am-midnight Sun-Thu, to 1am Fri & Sat, high tea 3-5.30pm Mon-Fri, noon-3pm & 3.30-6pm Sat & Sun; 📶; Ⓜ Raffles Place)

☑ Top Tip

Kopi Culture

Single-origin beans and the syphon brews may be all the rage among local hipsters, but Singapore's old-school *kopitiams* (coffeeshops) deliver the real local deal. Before heading in, it's a good idea to learn the lingo. *Kopi* means coffee with condensed milk, *kopi-o* is black coffee with sugar, while *kopi-c* gets you coffee with evaporated milk and sugar. If you need some cooling down, opt for a *kopi-peng* (iced coffee). Replace the word *kopi* with *teh* and you have the same variation for tea. One local tea concoction worth sipping is *teh tarik* – literally 'pulled tea' – a sweet spiced Indian tea.

Southbridge BAR

24 🚇 Map p30, D3

Rising above the glut of mediocre Boat Quay bars, this discerning rooftop hang-out delivers a panorama guaranteed to loosen jaws. Scan the skyline and river with a Lust, Caution cocktail (Sichuan pepper-infused gin, Cynar, lemon and soda), or taste-test an interesting selection of spirits that include Zacapa 23 Solera rum and Nikka Coffey Grain whisky. Entry is via the back alley, which runs off South Bridge Rd. (📞6877 6965; www.southbridge.sg; 5th fl, 80 Boat Quay; ⏰5-11.30pm; Ⓜ Clarke Quay)

ANDERS BLOMQVIST/GETTY IMAGES ©

Raffles Hotel

Lantern BAR

25 Map p30, E5

It may be lacking in height (it's dwarfed by the surrounding CBD buildings) and serve its drinks in plastic glasses (scandalous!), but Lantern remains a magical spot for a sophisticated evening toast. Why? There are the flickering lanterns, the shimmering, glass-sided pool (for **Fullerton Bay Hotel** (☎ 6333 8388; www.fullertonbayhotel.com; 80 Collyer Quay; r from S$600; ❋ @ ☎ ☎; **M** Raffles Place) guests only), and the romantic views over Marina Bay. (☎ 6597 5299; www.fullertonbayhotel.com; Fullerton Bay Hotel, 80 Collyer Quay; ⏰ 8am-1am Sun-Thu, to 2am Fri & Sat; **M** Raffles Place)

Raffles Hotel BAR

Granted, the prices are exorbitant, but there's something undeniably fabulous about an afternoon cocktail amid whitewashed colonial architecture and thick, tropical foliage at Raffles Hotel (see 5 Map p30, E2). Ditch the gloomy, clichéd **Long Bar** (⏰ 11am-12.30am Sun-Thu, to 1.30am Fri & Sat) for the fountain-graced **Raffles Courtyard** (www.raffleshotel.com; ⏰ noon-10.30pm) or sip Raj-style on the verandah at the **Bar & Billiard Room** (⏰ 5-11pm Tue-Thu, 5pm-1am Fri & Sat, noon-3pm Sun). Tip:

pass on the sickly-sweet Singapore sling for something more palatable, like the autumn sling. (6412 1816; www.raffles.com; 1 Beach Rd; City Hall)

Zouk

CLUB

26 Map p30, A3

Set to move to Clarke Quay (at Block C, The Cannery, River Valley Rd) in late 2016, Singapore's premier club draws some of the world's biggest DJs. Choose between the multilevel main club, the hip-hop-centric Phuture or the plush Velvet Underground, slung with original artworks by Andy Warhol, Frank Stella and Takashi Murakami. Take a taxi, and prepare to queue. (www.zoukclub.com; 17 Jiak Kim St; Zouk 11pm-late Wed, Fri & Sat, Phuture 10pm-late Wed, Fri & Sat, 9pm-3am Thu, Velvet Underground 10pm-late Wed, Fri & Sat, Wine Bar 6pm-2am Tue, 6pm-3am Wed & Thu, 6pm-4am Fri & Sat; 5, 16, 75, 175, 195, 970)

Level 33

MICROBREWERY

27 Map p30, E5

In a country obsessed with unique selling points, this one takes the cake – no, keg. Laying claim to being the world's highest 'urban craft brewery', Level 33 brews its own lager, pale ale, stout, porter and wheat beer. It's all yours to slurp alfresco with a jaw-dropping view over Marina Bay. Bargain hunters, take note: beers are cheaper before 8pm. (6834 3133; www.level33.com.sg; Level 33, Marina Bay Financial Tower 1, 8 Marina Blvd; noon-midnight Sun-Thu, noon-2am Fri & Sat; ; Downtown)

1-Altitude

BAR

28 Map p30, D4

Wedged across a triangle-shaped deck 282m above street level, this is the world's highest alfresco bar, its 360-degree panorama taking in soaring towers, colonial landmarks and a ship-clogged sea. Women enjoy free entry and all-night S$10 martinis on Wednesday, while Turn Back Thursday pumps out '80s, '90s and '00s hits. Dress up: no shorts or open shoes, gents. (6438 0410; www.1-altitude.com; Level 63, 1 Raffles Pl; admission incl 1 drink S$30; 6pm-2am Sun-Tue, to 3am Thu, to 4am Wed, Fri & Sat; Raffles Place)

Wine Connection

WINE BAR

29 Map p30, B2

Oenophiles love this savvy wine store and bar at Robertson Quay. The team works closely with winemakers across

Top Tip

Free Concerts

If you're hankering for wallet-friendly diversions, **Esplanade – Theatres on the Bay** (6828 8377; www.esplanade.com; 1 Esplanade Dr; box office noon-8.30pm; Esplanade, City Hall) offers free live performances on Friday, Saturday and Sunday that kick off around 7pm. The Singapore Symphony Orchestra (p44) performs free at the Singapore Botanic Gardens monthly. Check online for details.

the world, which means no intermediary. They have an interesting wine list and very palatable prices: glasses from S$7 and bottles as low as S$30. Edibles include decent salads and tartines, not to mention top-notch cheeses from their fabulously stinky, next-door Cheese Bar. (✆6235 5466; www.wineconnection.com.sg; 01-19/20 Robertson Walk, 11 Unity St; ⏱11.30am-1am Mon-Thu, to 2am Fri & Sat, to 11pm Sun; 📶; 🚌54, 64, 123, 139, 143, 186)

Entertainment

Singapore Symphony Orchestra
CLASSICAL MUSIC

30 ⭐ Map p30, F3

The 1800-seat state-of-the-art concert hall at the Esplanade – Theatres on the Bay is home to this respected orchestra, which also graces the Victoria Theatre & Concert Hall. It plays at least weekly; check the website or **SISTIC** (✆6348 5555; www.sistic.com.sg; Level 4 Concierge, ION Orchard, 2 Orchard Turn; Ⓜ Orchard) for details and book ahead. Student and senior (55-plus) discounts available; kids under six not permitted. (✆6602 4245; www.sso.org.sg; Esplanade – Theatres on the Bay, 1 Esplanade Dr; ⏱box office noon-8.30pm; Ⓜ Esplanade, City Hall)

Timbrè @ The Substation
LIVE MUSIC

31 ⭐ Map p30, D2

Young ones are content to queue for seats at this popular live-music venue, whose daily rotating roster features local bands and singer-songwriters playing anything from pop and rock to folk. Hungry punters can fill up on soups, salads, tapas and passable fried standbys like buffalo wings and truffle fries. (✆6338 8030; www.timbre.com.sg; 45 Armenian St; free with drink purchase; ⏱6pm-1am Sun-Thu, to 2am Fri & Sat; Ⓜ City Hall)

Singapore Chinese Orchestra
CLASSICAL MUSIC

32 ⭐ Map p30,

Using traditional instruments such as the liuqin, ruan and sanxian, the SCO treats listeners to classical Chinese concerts throughout the year. Concerts are held in various venues around the city, with occasional collaborations showcasing jazz musicians. (✆6557 4034; www.sco.com.sg; Singapore Conference Hall, 7 Shenton Way; ⏱8.30am-6pm Mon-Fri; Ⓜ Tanjong Pagar)

Singapore Repertory Theatre
THEATRE

33 ⭐ Map p30, B3

Based at the KC Arts Centre but also performing at other venues, the SRT produces international repertory standards as well as modern Singaporean plays. The company's annual Shakespeare in the Park series, enchantingly set in Fort Canning Park (p32), is deservedly popular. Check the website for upcoming productions. (✆6221 5585; www.srt.com.sg; KC Arts Centre, 20 Merbau Rd; 🚌54, 64, 123, 139, 143, 186, Ⓜ Clarke Quay)

Shopping

Kapok
GIFTS & SOUVENIRS

34  Map p30, E1

Inside the National Design Centre, Kapok showcases beautifully designed products from Singapore and beyond. Restyle your world with local jewellery from Myrrh, artisanal fragrances from Code Deco, and wristwatches from HyperGrand. Imports include anything from seamless Italian wallets to French tees and Nordic courier bags. When you're shopped out, recharge at the on-site cafe. (📞6339 7987; www.ka-pok.com; 01-05, National Design Centre, 111 Middle Rd; ⏰11am-9pm; Ⓜ Bugis)

Raffles Hotel Arcade
MALL

Part of the hotel complex, Raffles Hotel Arcade (see 5 Ⓒ Map p30, E2) is home to a handful of notable retailers. You'll find quality, affordable souvenirs (the vintage hotel posters are great buys) at **Raffles Hotel Gift Shop** (📞6337 1886; www.raffleshotelgifts.com; 01-01/03, Raffles Hotel Arcade, 1 Beach Rd; ⏰8.30am-9pm; Ⓜ City Hall) and high-end Singaporean art from emerging talent at **Chan Hampe** (📞6338 1962; www.chanhampegalleries.com; 01-2/021, Raffles Hotel Arcade, 328 North Bridge Rd; admission free; ⏰11am-7pm Tue-Sun; Ⓜ City Hall). And even if you can't afford its cameras, **Leica** (📞6336 9555; www.leica-store.sg; 01-18, Raffles Hotel Arcade, 328 North Bridge Rd; ⏰10am-8pm; Ⓜ City Hall) usually has a free, high-quality photographic exhibition on show. (www.raffles.com; 328 North Bridge Rd; Ⓜ City Hall)

Shoppes at Marina Bay Sands (p47)

Naiise
GIFTS & SOUVENIRS

35  Map p30, C3

Looking for unique and inspiring tokens of your time in Singapore? Put this airy, designer haven on your list. Cheeky postcards, fun local food prints, candy shaped cushions and even *nasi lemak* tea are available, along with beautiful homewares and accessories. These creative folk also run workshops; try your hand at calligraphy, book binding or concrete lamp making. (📞6702 3248; www.naiise.com; 02-23, Central, 6 Eu Tong Sen St; ⏰11am-10pm; Ⓜ Clarke Quay)

ANDREW WATSON/GETTY IMAGES ©

Understand

Architecture

Despite the wrecking-ball rampage of the 1960s and '70s, Singapore lays claim to a handful of heritage gems. An ever-expanding list of ambitious contemporary projects has the world watching.

Colonial Legacy

As the administrative HQ of British Malaya, Singapore gained a wave of buildings on a scale unprecedented in the colony. European aesthetics dominated, from the neoclassicism of City Hall, the Fullerton Building and the National Museum of Singapore to the Palladian-inspired Empress Building, now home to the Asian Civilisations Museum. While many other buildings adopted these styles, they were often tweaked to better suit the tropical climate, from the *porte cochère* (carriage porch) of St Andrew's Cathedral to the porticoes of the former St Joseph's Institution, current location of the Singapore Art Museum.

Shophouses

Singapore's narrow-fronted shophouses are among its most distinctive and charming architectural trademarks. Traditionally a ground-floor business topped by one or two residential floors, these contiguous blocks roughly span six styles from the 1840s to the 1960s. The true scene stealers are those built in the so-called Late Shophouse Style, with richly detailed facades often including colourful wall tiles, stucco flourishes, pilasters and elaborately shuttered windows. Fine examples grace Koon Seng Rd in Katong.

Singapore Now

Chinese American IM Pei is behind the iconic brutalist skyscraper OCBC Centre, the silvery Raffles City, and the razor-sharp Gateway twin towers. Britain's Sir Norman Foster designed the UFO-like Expo MRT station and Supreme Court, as well as the new South Beach mixed-use development (opposite Raffles Hotel), its two curving towers sliced with densely planted sky gardens. Designed by local studio Woha, the Parkroyal on Pickering hotel features dramatic hanging gardens, while Israeli-born Moshe Safdie's Marina Bay Sands turns heads with its record-breaking, 340m-long cantilevered Skypark.

Shoppes at
Marina Bay Sands   MALL

From Miu Miu pumps and Prada frocks to Boggi Milano blazers, this sprawling temple of aspiration at Marina Bay Sands (see 7 ⊙ Map p30, G5) gives credit cards a thorough workout. Despite being one of Singapore's largest luxury malls, it's relatively thin on crowds – great if you're not a fan of the Orchard Rd pandemonium. The world's first floating Louis Vuitton store is also here, right on Marina Bay. (☑6688 6888; www.marinabaysands.com; 10 Bayfront Ave; ⊙10.30am-11pm Sun-Thu, to 11.30pm Fri & Sat; 🛜; Ⓜ Bayfront)

Raffles City   MALL

36 🔒 Map p30, E2

Atrium-graced Raffles City includes a three-level branch of fashion-savvy Robinsons department store and a string of fashionable bag and luggage retailers, including Coach, Tumi and Kate Spade. You'll find kids' boutiques on level three. For high-end art by established and emerging Asian and Western artists, drop into **Ode to Art** (☑6250 1901; www.odetoart.com; 01-36, Raffles City, 252 North Bridge Rd; ⊙11am-9pm; Ⓜ City Hall) gallery. Hungry? Trawl the

decent basement food court. (☑6318 0238; www.rafflescity.com.sg; 252 North Bridge Rd; ⊙10am-10pm; 🛜; Ⓜ City Hall)

Redundant Shop   GIFTS & SOUVENIRS

37 🔒 Map p30, D2

Starting off tucked away inside a HDB estate, this port of call for Singaporean design lovers has hit the big time by moving to downtown Millenia Mall. Score svelte leather wallets from Holland's Secrid, scene-stealing socks from Swedish Happy Socks, old-school men's grooming range from New Zealand's Triumph & Disaster or all-weather tote bags from Massachusetts' Steele Canvas. (www.theredundantshop.com; 01-71/72, Millenia Walk, 9 Raffles Blvd; ⊙11am-9pm; Ⓜ Promenade, Esplanade)

Cathay Photo   ELECTRONICS

38 🔒 Map p30, D2

All the pros (and wannabes) shop at the extensively stocked Cathay Photo. **Peninsula Shopping Centre** across the road has several good secondhand camera stores. (☑6337 4274; www.cathayphoto.com.sg; 01-11, Peninsula Plaza, North Bridge Rd; ⊙10am-7pm Mon-Sat; Ⓜ City Hall)

Explore

Orchard Road

Shopping is Singapore's national sport and Orchard Rd is its Olympic-sized training ground. What was once a dusty road lined with spice plantations and orchards is now a torrent of malls, department stores and speciality shops; enough to burn out the toughest shopaholics. But wait, there's more, including drool-inducing food courts and a heritage-listed side street rocking with bars.

The Sights in a Day

☀ Breakfast late at **Kith Cafe** (p56) or retro **Killiney Kopitiam** (p55) before mall hopping on Orchard Rd. For regional fashion labels, check out **Hansel** (p60) as well as Sects and i.t., the latter two inside **Orchardgateway** (p59). For books, hit Kinokuniya inside **Ngee Ann City** (p60), then lose yourself inside futuristic **ION Orchard Mall** (p59). At the end of Orchard Rd, make a quick detour for prints at **Antiques of the Orient** (p59).

☀ Nibble exemplary *xiao long bao* (soup dumplings) at **Paradise Dynasty** (p54) or tuck into authentic Indonesian at **Tambuah Mas** (p54). Alternatively, save your appetite for high tea at **L'Espresso** (p57). If you're still on a retail high, shop **Paragon** (p59). If not, give your body some TLC at **Tomi Foot Reflexology** (p52) or (if booked ahead) **Remède Spa** (p52).

★ After 5pm, celebrate the good life with cut-price martinis at **Bar on 5** (p58), kick back at **Bar Canary** (p58) or drink among heritage buildings on Emerald Hill Rd. If you don't have a reservation at fine-dining **Iggy's** (p53) or **Buona Terra** (p53), refuel at Japanese-fusion It-kid **Kilo Orchard** (p55) or Hong Kong dumpling legend **Tim Ho Wan** (p54).

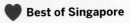 **Best of Singapore**

Shopping
ION Orchard Mall (p59)

Tanglin Shopping Centre (p59)

Paragon (p59)

Sects (p59)

Food
Iggy's (p53)

Buona Terra (p53)

Gordon Grill (p54)

Paradise Dynasty (p54)

Drinking
Manhattan (p57)

L'Espresso (p57)

Getting There

Ⓜ **MRT** Orchard Rd is served by no less than three MRT stations: Orchard (Red Line), Somerset (Red Line) and Dhoby Ghaut (Red, Purple and Yellow Lines). There's really no need to use any other form of transport to get here.

A **B** **C** **D**

1

6 Scotts Rd

Anderson Rd

Orange Grove Rd

Draycott Rd

Draycott Dr

Claymore Hill

18

9

21

Claymore Rd

2

Tanglin Rd

23

Orchard Rd

28

Cuscaden Rd

7

Claymore Rd

Scotts Rd

Nutmeg Rd

26

Mount Elizabeth

2

Remède Spa

17

Tomlinson Rd

Orchard Blvd

31

4 Tomi Foot Reflexology

3

8 22

M
Orchard

15

10 24

Orchard Rd

Paterson Rd

Anguillia Park

Orchard Turn

Orchard Blvd

29

Orchard Link

20

Jln Tupai

4

Jln Kelawar

Jln Arnap

Paterson Hill

Paterson Rd

Grange Rd

Grange Rd

Hoot Kiam Rd

Irwell Bank Rd

Leonie Hill

Leonie Hill Rd

Leonie Hill

St Thomas Walk

River Valley Rd

5

E   F   G   H

1

Anthony Rd

Peck Hay Rd

Monk's Hill Rd

Clemenceau Ave Nth

Clemenceau Rise

Cairnhill Rd

Cavenagh Rd

Istana Park

3 ⊙
Istana

500 m

0.25 miles

Bukit Timah Rd

Mackenzie Rd

2

Cairnhill Circle

...eford Rd

Cairnhill Rd

Saunders Rd

Emerald Hill Rd

Central Expwy

1 ⊙
Hullet Rd
**Emerald Hill
Road**

Mt Emily
Park

Upper Wilkie Rd

Wilkie Rd

Mt Sophia Rd

3

30 🔒

Singapore
Visitors Centre
@ Orchard ℹ

🔒
27

313@Somerset 🔒 **25** 🔒 ✕**12**

Ⓜ
Somerset

Buyong Rd

Kramat Rd

Keok Rd

Kramat Ln

Orchard Rd

Penang Rd

Edinburgh Rd

Oldham La

11
✕

Cathay
Gallery
5 ⊙

4

Handy Rd

Exeter Rd

Eber Rd

✕**13**

Devonshire Rd

Killiney Rd

Lloyd Rd

Oxley Rd

Oxley Rise

Clemenceau Ave

Penang La

Ⓜ Dhoby
Ghaut

14 ✕

Fort Canning Rd

Fort
Canning
Park

5

Sights

Emerald Hill Road ARCHITECTURE

1 ◎ Map p50, F3

Take time out from your shopping to wander up frangipani-scented Emerald Hill Rd, graced with some of Singapore's finest terrace houses. Look out for No 56 (built in 1902, and one of the earliest buildings here), Nos 39 to 45 (with unusually wide frontages and a grand Chinese-style entrance gate), and Nos 120 to 130 (with art deco features dating from around 1925). At the Orchard Rd end of the hill is a cluster of popular bars in fetching shophouse renovations. (Emerald Hill Rd; ⓂSomerset)

Remède Spa SPA

2 ◎ Map p50, A2

Reputed to have the best masseurs in town, the St Regis Hotel's in-house spa is also home to the award-winning Pedi:Mani:Cure Studio by renowned pedicurist Bastien Gonzalez. Remède's wet lounge – a marbled wonderland of steam room, sauna, ice fountains and spa baths – is a perfect prelude to standout treatments like the 90-minute warm jade stone massage (S$290). (☑6506 6896; www.remedespasingapore. com; St Regis Hotel, 29 Tanglin Rd; 1hr massage from S$180; ◷9am-midnight; ⓂOrchard)

Istana PALACE

3 ◎ Map p50, G2

The grand, whitewashed, neoclassical home of Singapore's president, set in

16 hectares of grounds, was built by the British between 1867 and 1869 as Government House, and is open to visitors five times a year: on Labour Day (1 May), a chosen date before National Day (7 August), Chinese New Year (January or February), Diwali (October or November) and Hari Raya Puasa (or Eid-ul Fitr, the festival marking the end of Ramadan; dates vary). Check website to confirm. (www. istana.gov.sg; Orchard Rd; grounds/palace S$2/4; ◷8.30am-6pm, open days only; ⓂDhoby Ghaut)

Tomi Foot Reflexology MASSAGE

4 ◎ Map p50, D3

Yes, that's Sting in the photo – even he knows about this no-frills massage joint, lurking in 1970s throwback Lucky Plaza. Head in for one of the best rubdowns in town, provided by a tactile team in matching pink polos. Techniques include acupressure and shiatsu, all approved by Jesus and Mary, hanging on the wall. (☑6736 4249; 01-94 Lucky Plaza, 304 Orchard Rd; 30min foot reflexology S$30; ◷10am-10pm; ⓂOrchard)

Cathay Gallery MUSEUM

5 ◎ Map p50, H4

Film and nostalgia buffs will appreciate this pocket-sized silver-screen museum, housed in Singapore's first high-rise building. The displays trace the history of the Loke family, early pioneers in film production and distribution in Singapore and founders

Colourful terraced houses, Emerald Hill Road

of the Cathay Organisation. Highlights include old movie posters, cameras and programs that capture the golden age of local cinema. (www.thecathaygallery.com.sg; 02-16 The Cathay, 2 Handy Rd; admission free; ⏰11am-7pm Mon-Sat; Ⓜ Dhoby Ghaut)

Eating

Buona Terra
ITALIAN $$$

6 🍴 Map p50, D1

This intimate, linen-lined Italian is one of Singapore's unsung glories. In the kitchen is young Lombard chef Denis Lucchi, who turns exceptional ingredients into elegant, modern dishes, like seared duck liver with poached peach, amaretti crumble and Vin Santo ice cream. Lucchi's right-hand man is Emilian sommelier Gabriele Rizzardi, whose wine list, though expensive, is extraordinary. (📞6733 0209; www.buonaterra.com.sg; 29 Scotts Rd; 3-course set lunch S$38, 3-/4-/5-course dinner S$88/108/128; ⏰noon-2.30pm & 6.30-10.30pm Mon-Fri, 6.30-10.30pm Sat; 🛜; Ⓜ Newton)

Iggy's
FUSION $$$

7 🍴 Map p50, B2

Iggy's dark, slinky design promises something special, and head chef Masahiro Isono delivers with his arresting, poetic takes on fusion flavours. Menus are tweaked according to season, though the knock-out capellini with *sakura ebi* (shrimp), *konbu* (kelp) and shellfish oil is always on call to blow gastronomes away. Superlatives extend to the wine list, one of the city's finest. (☎6732 2234; www.iggys.com.sg; Level 3, Hilton Hotel, 581 Orchard Rd; 3-course lunch S\$85-150, set dinner menus S\$195-275; ☉noon-1.30pm (last seating) & 7-9.30pm (last seating) Mon, Tue & Thu-Sat; ✍; Ⓜ Orchard)

Paradise Dynasty　　CHINESE \$\$

8 ✗ Map p50, C3

Preened staffers in headsets whisk you into this svelte dumpling den, passing a glassed-in kitchen where Chinese chefs stretch their noodles and steam their buns. Skip the novelty-flavoured *xiao long bao* (soup dumplings) for the original version, which arguably beat those of legendary competitor Din Tai Fung. Beyond these, standouts include *la mian* (hand-pulled noodles) with buttery, braised pork belly. www.paradisegroup.com.sg; 04-12A ION Orchard, 2 Orchard Turn; dishes S\$4-25; ☉11am-10pm Mon-Fri, from 10.30am Sat & Sun; Ⓜ Orchard)

Gordon Grill　　INTERNATIONAL \$\$\$

9 ✗ Map p50, D2

With its old-world charm, complete with crisp linens and its famed steaks, Gordon Grill, housed inside this colonial-era hotel, is a step back in time compared with ultramodern Orchard Rd. It's as much an experience as it is a meal, so this is perhaps the best place for splashing out on

the wagyu beef, ordered by weight, cut at your table and cooked to your specifications.

The weekend roast lunch is immensely popular, so book well in advance. (☎6730 1744; www.goodwoodparkhotel.com; Goodwood Park Hotel, 22 Scotts Rd; mains S\$44-62; ☉noon-2.30pm & 7-10.30pm; Ⓜ Orchard)

Tambuah Mas　　INDONESIAN \$\$

10 ✗ Map p50, D3

Hiding shyly in a corner of Paragon's food-packed basement, Tambuah Mas is where Indonesian expats head for a taste of home. Bright, modern and good value for Orchard Rd, it proudly makes much of what it serves from scratch, a fact evident in what could possibly be Singapore's best beef *rendang*. No reservations, so arrive early if dining Thursday to Saturday. (☎6733 2220; www.tambuahmas.com.sg; B1-44 Paragon, 290 Orchard Rd; mains S\$7.50-29; ☉11am-10pm; ☏; Ⓜ Orchard)

Tim Ho Wan　　DIM SUM \$\$

11 ✗ Map p50, G4

Hong Kong's Michelin-starred dim-sum seller is steaming in Singapore, with the same Mong Kok queues (head in after 8.30pm) and tick-the-boxes order form. While nothing compares to the original (the Singapore branches need to import many ingredients), the recipes are the same and the results still pretty spectacular. Must-trys include the sugary buns with barbecue pork and the perky prawn dumplings. (☎6251 2000; www.

Understand
Black & Whites

Often seen peeking through the lush, forested corners of Singapore, these distinctive black and white bungalows are a reminder of Singapore's colonial past. Usually built by wealthy plantation owners between the late 19th century and WWII, these grand homes have retained the character and charm of days gone by. The design itself was greatly influenced by the Arts and Craft movement. Originating in England in the 1860s, the movement placed renewed value on craftsmanship, a counter reaction to England's rapid industrialisation.

Once there were 10,000 of these beauties in Singapore, but after being left derelict post-war, approximately only 500 remain. The majority are now owned by the government and are regarded as national monuments; however, some are rented to families and businesses. While incredibly popular with the expat community for their large gardens and airy interiors (rare to find in space-constrained Singapore), rental costs are hefty and hopeful tenants must bid to secure two-year leases.

Some Black & Whites are occasionally opened to the public, but the easiest way to see inside one is to join a tour with Geraldene Lowe-Ismail (www.geraldenestours.com), whose fascinating stories transport you back to colonial Singapore. Alternatively, a number of restaurants call these properties home – you'll find several along Scotts Rd. If you're in the mood for a fancy Italian dinner our pick is Buona Terra (p53).

timhowan.com; 01-29 Plaza Singapura, 68 Orchard Rd; dishes from S$3.80; ◷10am-10pm Mon-Fri, 9am-10pm Sat & Sun; Ⓜ Dhoby Ghaut)

Kilo Orchard
FUSION $$

12 Ⓧ Map p50, F4

Tucked away in PACT, a multi-shop retail space, this industrial-styled hot spot dishes up sublime Japanese fusion to ravenous Orchard Rd shoppers. If you stop for lunch, order off the bowl menu; our pick is the pork belly with brown rice. Super hungry?

Wolf down a Smashburger. At dinner, don't go past the barbecue pork riblets, which are falling-off-the-bone good. (☏6884 7560; www.kilokitchen.com; 02-16/18 Orchard Central, 181 Orchard Rd; mains S$16-33; ◷11.30am-3pm & 5.30-10pm Mon-Sat, 11am-6pm Sun; Ⓜ Somerset)

Killiney Kopitiam
CAFE $

13 Ⓧ Map p50, F4

Start the day the old-school way at this veteran coffee joint, pimped with endearingly lame laminated jokes. Order a strong *kopi* (coffee), a serve of *kaya* (coconut jam) toast and a side of soft-boiled egg. Crack open the latter, add a dash of soy sauce and pepper, then dip your *kaya* toast in it. (☑6734 3910; www.killiney-kopitiam.com; 67 Killiney Rd; dishes S\$0.90-6.90; ⏱6am-11pm Mon & Wed-Sat, to 6pm Tue & Sun; Ⓜ Somerset)

Kith Café
CAFE \$\$

14 ❌ Map p50, H5

Kith kicks butt on several levels. It opens when many Singapore cafes are still snoozing, it offers free wi-fi and cool magazines, the coffee is good (it has soy milk!), and the grub is fresh and tasty. All-day breakfast items span

Local Life
Food Court Flavours

Burrow into the basement of most malls on Orchard Rd and you'll find a food court with stall upon stall selling cheap, freshly cooked dishes from all over the world. One of the best is slick, sprawling **Takashimaya Food Village** (Map p50, D3; ☑65-6506 0458; www.takashimaya.com.sg; B2 Takashimaya Department Store, Ngee Ann City, 391 Orchard Rd; dishes S\$4-17; ⏱10am-9.30pm; Ⓜ Orchard), which serves up a who's who of Japanese, Korean and other Asian culinary classics. Look out for *soon kueh* (steamed dumplings stuffed with bamboo shoots, bangkwang, dried mushroom, carrot and dried prawn), and don't miss a fragrant bowl of noodles from the Tsuru-koshi stand.

virtuous muesli to cheeky egg-based slap-ups, and both the salads and sandwiches pique interest with their gourmet combos. (☑6338 8611; http://kith.com.sg; 01-01 Park Mall, 9 Penang Rd; dishes S\$7-24; ⏱8am-10pm Tue-Sun; 🛜✍; Ⓜ Dhoby Ghaut)

Food Republic
FOOD COURT \$

15 ❌ Map p50, C3

A cornucopia of street food in air-conditioned comfort. Muck in with the rest of the crowd for seats before joining the longest queues for dishes spanning Japan, Korea and Thailand, to India, Indonesia and, quite rightly, Singapore. (☑6737 9881; www.foodrepublic.com.sg; Level 4, Wisma Atria, 435 Orchard Rd; dishes S\$4-15; ⏱10am-10pm; 🛜; Ⓜ Orchard)

Wild Honey
CAFE \$\$

16 ❌ Map p50, E4

With industrial-style windows, concrete floors and plush designer furniture, Wild Honey feels airy and contemporary. It serves scrumptious all-day breakfasts from around the world, from smoked salmon–laced Norwegian to *shakshuka*-spiced Tunisian. Other options include muesli, gourmet sandwiches and freshly roasted coffee. Consider booking a day in advance if heading in on weekends, when it gets busy. (☑6235 3900; www.wildhoney.com.sg; 03-02 Mandarin Gallery, 333A Orchard Rd; dishes S\$12-35; ⏱9am-9.30pm Sun-Thu, to 10.30pm Fri & Sat; ✍; Ⓜ Somerset)

PETER HORREE/ALAMY ©

Diners at Food Republic

Drinking

Manhattan
BAR

17 🚇 Map p50, A3

Step back in time to the golden age of fine drinking at this handsome *Mad Men*-esque bar, where long-forgotten cocktails come back to life. Grouped by New York neighbour-hoods, drink highlights include the woody 'eight ward' and the fun 'box office smash', which is served with a side of popcorn. (☎6725 3377; www.regenthotels.com/en/Singapore; Level 2, Regent, 1 Cuscaden Rd; ⏱5pm-1am, Sunday cocktail brunch 11.30am-3.30pm; MOrchard)

L'Espresso
LOUNGE

18 🚇 Map p50, D1

The place to be seen to 'tea', this bright and airy lobby lounge, with poolside terrace, is the perfect spot to end a day of Orchard Rd shopping. The crockery is dainty, cream clotted, staff sharply attired and each bite-sized morsel delicately presented. Sink into a leather lounge chair, sip your tea and see if you can resist heading back to the buffet just one last time. (☎6730 1743; www.goodwoodparkhotel.com; Goodwood Park Hotel, 22 Scotts Rd; high tea adult/child Mon-Thu S$45/22.50, Fri-Sun S$48/24; ⏱10am-midnight, high tea 2-5.30pm Mon-Thu, noon-2.30pm & 3-5.30pm Fri-Sun; 🛜; MOrchard)

Local Life
Emerald Hill Road

Housed in century-old Peranakan shophouses, Emerald Hill Road's cluster of bars are popular with the after-work crowd. Top billing goes to neon-pimped **Ice Cold Beer** (Map p51, E3; ✆6735 9929; www.ice-cold-beer. com; 9 Emerald Hill Rd; ⊙5pm-2am Sun-Thu, to 3am Fri & Sat; Ⓜ Somerset), a raucous, boozy dive bar with dart boards, a pool table and tongue-in-cheek soft-core pinups on the wall. It's a come-as-you-are kind of place where you don't have to be 20-something to have a rocking good time. Good happy hour deals run from 5pm to 9pm, and it's especially kicking on Friday nights.

Bar Canary   BAR

19 🍺 Map p50, D3

Canary-yellow beanbags, artificial turf and the sound of humming traffic and screeching birds – alfresco Bar Canary hovers high above frenetic Orchard Rd. It's fab for an evening tipple, with well-positioned fans. Book at least a week ahead for its Wednesday Girls' Night Out: S$50, plus tax, for free-flow champagne, house wines, spirits and signature cocktails from 7pm to 9pm (S$100 for guys). (✆6603 8855; www. parkhotelgroup.com/orchard; Park Hotel Orchard, 270 Orchard Rd, entry on Bideford Rd; ⊙noon-1am Sun-Thu, to 2am Fri & Sat; 📶; Ⓜ Somerset)

Bar on 5   BAR

20 🍺 Map p50, D4

This slinky hotel bar has one of the best happy hour deals in town: smooth, well-crafted martinis for under S$10 a pop. Purists should forego the flavoured versions on the menu and request a classic dry instead. Drink specials run from 5pm to 9pm, accompanied by a largely middle-management crowd and eclectic tunes spanning ABBA to Rihanna. (✆6831 6286; www.bar-on-5.com.sg; Level 5, Mandarin Orchard, 333 Orchard Rd; ⊙11am-1am Sun-Thu, to 2am Fri & Sat; Ⓜ Somerset)

Entertainment

TAB   LIVE MUSIC

21 ⭐ Map p50, B2

Looking slicker after a revamp, TAB opens each night for Club SONAR, which serves up either DJ club sets or live-music acts from across Asia. The venue also hosts ticketed concerts once or twice a month, featuring established and up-and-coming talent. (✆6493 6952; www.tab.com. sg; 02-29 Orchard Hotel, 442 Orchard Rd; ⊙Club SONAR 9.30pm-5.30am Sun-Thu, to 6am Fri & Sat; Ⓜ Orchard)

Shopping

ION Orchard Mall MALL

22 🔒 Map p50, C3

Rising directly above Orchard MRT station, futuristic ION is the cream of Orchard Rd malls. Basement floors focus on mere-mortal high-street labels like Zara and Uniqlo, while upper-floor tenants read like the index of *Vogue*. Dining options span food-court bites to posher nosh, and the attached 56-storey tower offers a top-floor viewing gallery, **ION Sky** (6238 8228; Level 56, ION Orchard, 2 Orchard Turn; admission free; ⏱3-6pm, last entry 5.30pm). (www.ionorchard.com; 430 Orchard Rd; ⏱10am-10pm; MOrchard)

Tanglin Shopping Centre MALL

23 🔒 Map p50, A2

This retro mall specialises in Asian art and is *the* place to come for quality rugs, carvings, ornaments, jewellery, paintings, furniture and the like. Top billing goes to **Antiques of the Orient** (6734 9351; www.aoto.com.sg; ⏱10am-5.30pm Mon-Sat, 11am-3.30pm Sun; MOrchard), with original and reproduction prints, photographs, and maps of Singapore and Asia. Especially beautiful are the richly hued botanical drawings commissioned by British colonist William Farquhar. (6737 0849; www.tanglinsc.com; 19 Tanglin Rd; ⏱10am-10pm; MOrchard)

Paragon MALL

24 🔒 Map p50, D3

Even if you don't have a Black AmEx, strike a pose inside this Maserati of Orchard Rd malls. Status labels include Burberry, Prada, Jimmy Choo and Gucci. High-street brands include Banana Republic and G-Star Raw. (6738 5535; www.paragon.com.sg; 290 Orchard Rd; ⏱10am-9pm; 📶; MSomerset)

Orchardgateway MALL

25 🔒 Map p50, E4

Occupying a position on both sides of Orchard Rd, conveniently linked by an underground and above-ground walkway, this mall is home to boundary-pushing fashion stores **Sects Shop** (9889 2179; www.sectss-shop.com; 04-14 Orchardgateway, 218 Orchard Rd; ⏱11am-10pm Sun-Fri, to 10.30pm Sat; MSomerset) and **i.t** (6702 7186; www.itlabels.com.sg; B1-13 & 01-18 Orchardgateway, 277 Orchard Rd; ⏱11am-9.30pm; MSomerset). Fellas head to level four, where you'll find unique fashion and accessories tailored to discerning gentlemen. (6513 4633; www.orchardgateway.sg; 277 & 218 Orchard Rd; ⏱10.30am-10.30pm; MSomerset)

Pedder On Scotts SHOES

26 🔒 Map p50, C2

Even if you're not in the market for high-end heels and bags, Pedder On Scotts thrills with its creative, whimsical items. The store hand picks only the most unique pieces from leading designers, and displays them in separate 'zones' – each more creative than the next. Accessories include statement jewellery fit for a modern gallery. (📞 6244 2883; www.pedderon-scotts.com; Level 2, Scotts Sq, 6 Scotts Rd; ⏱10am-10pm; Ⓜ Orchard)

Hansel
FASHION & ACCESSORIES

27 🔒 Map p50, E4

Fashion-savvy women shouldn't miss Hansel, domain of local designer Jo Soh and her chic, playful, vintage-inspired creations. (📞 6836 5367; www.ilovehansel.com; 02-14 Mandarin Gallery, 333A Orchard Rd; ⏱noon-8pm Mon-Thu, till 9pm Fri-Sat; Ⓜ Somerset)

Understand
Thai'd to Tradition

With new shopping malls being shoehorned into every available space on Orchard Rd, why, many visitors ask, does the Thai embassy occupy such large, prominent grounds in an area of staggeringly expensive real estate? Back in the 1990s, the Thai government was reportedly offered S$139 million for the site, but turned it down because selling the land, bought by Thailand for S$9000 in 1983 by the revered King Chulalongkorn (Rama V), would be seen as an affront to his memory. And so, it remains, drooled over by frustrated developers.

Forum
MALL

28 🔒 Map p50, B2

Peaceful, light-filled Forum eschews obvious brands for more discerning offerings. Deep-pocketed, fashion-forward women browse the racks at TriBeCa (stocks Rachel Zoe and Anna Sui), while fashion-literate guys and girls bag hip, make-a-statement threads and footwear at **Club 21b** (📞 6304 1455; www.club21global.com; ⏱10am-8pm Mon-Sat, 10.30am-6pm Sun). One floor up is a string of boutiques dedicated to designer kids' clothing and quality toys. (📞 6732 2469; www.forumtheshoppingmall.com.sg; 583 Orchard Rd; ⏱10am-9pm; Ⓜ Orchard)

Ngee Ann City
MALL

29 🔒 Map p50, D3

It might look like a forbidding mau-soleum, but this marble-and-granite behemoth promises retail giddiness on its seven floors. International luxury brands compete for space with sprawling bookworm nirvana **Kinokuniya** (📞 6737 5021; www.kinokuniya.com.sg; ⏱10am-9.30pm Sun-Fri, to 10pm Sat) and upmarket Japanese department store **Takashimaya** (📞 6506 0458; www.takashimaya.com.sg; ⏱10am-9.30pm), home to Takashimaya Food Village, one of the strip's best food courts. (📞 6506 0461; www.ngeeanncity.com.sg; 391 Orchard Rd; ⏱10am-9.30pm, restaurants till 11pm; Ⓜ Somerset)

ION Orchard Mall (p59)

Robinsons
DEPARTMENT STORE

30 🔒 Map p50, E3

The flagship for Singapore's top department store offers sharp fashion edits, pairing well-known 'It' labels like Emporio Armani, Ted Baker and Marc Jacobs with street-smart cognoscenti brands, such as Brownbreath and Saturdays NYC. Clothes and kicks aside, you'll find anything from Shinola Detroit leathergoods to Balmain bedlinen. (📞6735 8838; www.robinsons.com.sg; 260 Orchard Rd; 🕙10.30am-10pm; Ⓜ Somerset)

Tangs
DEPARTMENT STORE

31 🔒 Map p50, C3

Since opening its doors more than 70 years ago, Tangs has become a Singaporean institution. This five-floor department store is popular with all generations, selling business suits, formal evening attire and streetwear in the huge clothes section, as well as electronics, shoes and some of the best homewares in town. (📞6737 5500; www.tangs.com; 320 Orchard Rd; 🕙10.30am-9.30pm Mon-Sat, 11am-8.30pm Sun; 📶; Ⓜ Orchard)

Local Life
Tiong Bahru

Getting There

Ⓜ **MRT** Catch the metro to Tiong Bahru, walk east along Tiong Bahru Rd for 350m, then turn right into Kim Pong Rd.

Spend a weekend morning in Tiong Bahru, Singapore's epicentre of independent cool. An easy three stops from Raffles Place MRT station, it's more than just an ever-increasing list of eclectic boutiques, bookstores, cafes and bakeries that make this low-rise neighbourhood worth a saunter. This area was Singapore's first public housing estate, its streetscape of walk-up, art deco apartments now among the city's most unexpected architectural treats.

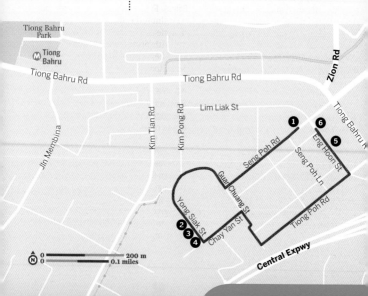

❶ Market & Food Centre

The **Tiong Bahru Market & Food Centre** (83 Seng Poh Rd; dishes from S$3; ⊙8am-late, individual stalls vary; Ⓜ Tiong Bahru) remains staunchly old-school, down to its orange-hued exterior, the neighbourhood's original shade. Its hawker centre is home to cultish **Jian Bo Shui Kueh** (shui kueh from S$2; ⊙7am-9pm), famous for its *chwee kueh* (steamed rice cake with diced preserved radish).

❷ BooksActually

Bibliophilic bliss, **BooksActually** (☎6222 9195; www.booksactually.com; 9 Yong Siak St; ⊙10am-8pm Tue-Sat, to 6pm Mon & Sun; Ⓜ Tiong Bahru) is Singapore's coolest independent bookstore, with an unusual range of fiction and nonfiction, including some interesting titles on Singapore. For beautiful children's books, check out **Woods in the Books** (☎6222 9980; www.woodsin-thebooks.sg; 3 Yong Siak St; ⊙11am-8pm Tue-Sat, to 6pm Sun; Ⓜ Tiong Bahru), three doors down.

❸ Strangelets

Strangelets (☎6222 1456; www.strange-lets.sg; 7 Yong Siak St; ⊙11am-8pm Mon-Fri, 10am-8pm Sat & Sun; Ⓜ Tiong Bahru) is an attractively curated design store filled with quirky local jewellery, French candles, Florentine soaps, Swedish socks, Californian bags and rucksacks. Try the lychee beet organic Popaganda popsicles.

❹ Nana & Bird

A few shops up is **Nana & Bird** (☎9117 0430; http://shop.nanaandbird.com; 1M Yong Siak St; ⊙noon-7pm Mon-Fri, 11am-7pm Sat & Sun; Ⓜ Tiong Bahru). Originally a pop-up concept store, it's now a Tiong Bahru staple, with forward fashion, accessories and art. Find unexpected labels including Singapore's Aijek and Ylin Lu, and international up-and-comers Kuwaii and Peggy Hartanto.

❺ Tiong Bahru Bakery

Get some French lovin' at baker Gontran Cherrier's cool, contemporary **Tiong Bahru Bakery** (☎6220 3430; www.tiongbahrubakery.com; 01-70, 56 Eng Hoon St; pastries S$3-8, sandwiches from S$8; ⊙8am-8pm Sun-Thu, to 10pm Fri & Sat; Ⓜ Tiong Bahru). Faultless pastries include buttery almond brioche, while savouries include salubrious sandwiches exploding with prime ingredients. Topping it off is beautiful coffee from Common Man Roasters.

❻ We Need a Hero

Blokes: if you're feeling rough around the edges, plonk yourself down in one of the old-school barber chairs and let the **We Need a Hero** (☎6222 5590; www.weneedahero.sg; 01-86, 57 Eng Hoon St; barber cut from S$45, shave from S$35; ⊙11am-9pm Mon-Fri, from 10am Sat, 10am-8pm Sun; Ⓜ Tiong Bahru) team unleash their grooming superpowers. All bases are covered, from basic shaves and cuts, to rejuvenating face masks and soothing massages.

Explore

Chinatown & the CBD

These 'hoods deliver diverse architecture, culinary riches and high-cred bars. Not huge on must-see sights, it's mainly about the vibe. Dive into Chinatown for wet markets, hawker food and temples, and into the CBD to party atop a skyscraper and in a converted bank. South of Chinatown, Tanjong Pagar lures with galleries, artisan coffee, cocktails and heritage shophouses.

The Sights in a Day

☀️ Breakfast at veteran **Ya Kun Kaya Toast** (p78), then get the dirt on the area's past at the **Chinatown Heritage Centre** (p"Chinatown Heritage Centre" on page 66). Picture those opium dens as you saunter down Pagoda St to colour-bursting **Sri Mariamman Temple** (p72). Bag a local artwork at **Utterly Art** (p83) or some Chinese remedies at **Eu Yan Sang** (p83).

☀️ Score a table at **Maxwell Food Centre** (p75) to taste-test Singapore's legendary street food, then find tranquillity in a rooftop garden at the epic **Buddha Tooth Relic Temple** (p72). Make your way to **Tea Chapter** (p81) for old-fashioned tea and nibbles. Alternatively, treat yourself to a little cut-price reflexology at **People's Park Complex** (p74).

🌙 Come dinner, opt for melt-in-your-mouth meat at hot-spot **Burnt Ends** (p74), killer crab at **Momma Kong's** (p74) or contemporary Southeast Asian flavours at **Ding Dong** (p75). Fed, end the evening sampling some of Singapore's top cocktail bars, among them **Operation Dagger** (p78), **Tippling Club** (p78) and **Spiffy Dapper** (p79), or catch a rooftop breeze at tiki-tastic **Potato Head Folk** (p78).

For a local's day in Chinatown, see p68.

👁 Top Sights

Chinatown Heritage Centre (p66)

🔍 Local Life

Chinatown Tastebuds & Temples (p68)

❤️ Best of Singapore

Museums
Chinatown Heritage Centre (p66)

Baba House (p72)

Food
Burnt Ends (p74)

Momma Kong's (p74)

Drinking
Operation Dagger (p78)

Tippling Club (p78)

Getting There

Ⓜ **MRT** Alight at Chinatown (Purple and Blue Lines) for Chinatown, Raffles Place (Red and Green Lines) or the CBD and Telok Ayer for Amoy St and Club Street. Tanjong Pagar (Green Line) and Outram Park (Purple and Green Lines) are best for Duxton Hill.

🚌 **Bus** The 61, 145 and 166 link Chinatown to the Colonial District.

Top Sights
Chinatown Heritage Centre

The Chinatown Heritage Centre lifts the lid on Chinatown's chaotic, colourful and often scandalous past. Its endearing jumble of old photographs, personal anecdotes and recreated environments deliver an evocative stroll through the neighbourhood's highs and lows. Spend some time in here and you'll see Chinatown's now tourist-conscious streets in a much more intriguing light.

Map p70, D2

6224 3928

www.chinatownheritagecentre.com.sg

48 Pagoda St

adult/child under 13yr S$15/10

9am-8pm, closed 1st Mon each month

M Chinatown

Don't Miss

Tailor Shop & Living Quarters

The journey back to old Singapore begins on the ground floor with a recreated tailor shop-front, workshop and cramped living quarters of the tailor's family and apprentices. By the early 1950s, Pagoda St was heaving with tailor shops and this is an incredibly detailed replica of what was once a common neighbourhood fixture.

Recreated Cubicles

Time travel continues on the 1st floor. Faithfully designed according to the memories and stories of former residents, a row of cubicles will have you peering into the ramshackle living quarters of opium-addicted coolies, stoic Samsui women and even a family of eight! It's a powerful sight, vividly evoking the tough, grim lives that many of the area's residents endured right up to the mid-20th century. Keep your eyes peeled for the vermin (don't worry, it's fake) in every cubicle.

Early Pioneer Exhibits

The flashy new top floor invites you to join the perilous journey Chinese immigrants under-took to reach Singapore, and to discover the customs, cuisine and importance of family net-works when they arrived, via a range of sensory exhibits. Many new arrivals fell victim to gambling rings and opium dealers; see the pipes and tiles that they used to lose their minds and their money. One street that you won't want to go down is Sago Lane (Street of the Dead), a sombre but fascinating glimpse into what oc-curred during a person's time of expiration.

☑ Top Tips

▶ Allow yourself at least 1½ hours to see and experience all the exhibits, more if you're a history buff.

▶ Aim to arrive just after opening – the museum is physically very small so best to beat the crowds.

▶ Keep your nostrils on alert – you may get a whiff of some old China-town smells.

✗ Take a Break

If you arrive before open-ing time, join the locals at **Nanyang Old Coffee** (☏ 6100 3450; www.nanyang-goldcoffee.com; 268 South Bridge Rd; toast sets S$4.30, kopi from S$1.50; ◷7am-6pm; Ⓜ Chinatown) for a traditional breakfast set of *kaya* (coconut jam) toast, runny eggs and strong *kopi* (coffee).

For tasty local fare, head to Chinatown Complex, a labyrinth of hawker stalls. The wait for mixed claypot rice at Lian He Ben Ji Claypot Rice (p76) is worth it.

Local Life
Chinatown Tastebuds & Temples

Considering its past as a hotpot of opium dens, death houses and brothels, it's easy to write off today's Chinatown as a paler version of its former self. Yet beyond the tourist tack that chokes Pagoda, Temple and Trengganu Sts lies a still-engrossing neighbourhood where life goes on as it has for generations, at cacophonous market stalls, retro *kopitiams* (coffee-shops) and historic temples.

1 Chinatown Wet Market

Elbow aunties at the famous **Chinatown Wet Market** (11 New Bridge Rd; ⊙5am–noon; MChinatown), in the basement of the Chinatown Complex. At its best early in the morning, it's a rumble-inducing feast of wriggling seafood, exotic fruits and vegetables, Chinese spices and preserved goods.

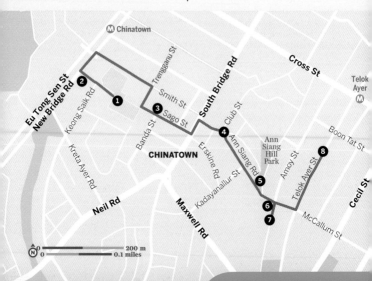

2 Tiong Shian Porridge Centre

Appetite piqued, pull up a plastic stool at **Tiong Shian Porridge Centre** (☎6222 3911; 265 New Bridge Rd; porridge S$3.50-8; ◷24hr; MChinatown), an old-school *kopitiam* where old uncles tuck into delicious congee. Winners here include porridge with century egg and pork, and the speciality claypot frog leg porridge. Each order is made fresh.

3 Chop Tai Chong Kok

Pick up something sweet at **Chop Tai Chong Kok** (☎6227 5701; www.taichongkok.com; 34 Sago St; pastries from S$1; ◷9.30am-6pm Mon, to 8pm Tue-Sun; MChinatown), a super-traditional pastry shop in business since 1938. If you're undecided, opt for the speciality lotus-paste mooncakes. Once known for its sago factories and brothels, Sago St itself now sells everything from barbecued meat to pottery.

4 Ann Siang Road & Club Street

A quick walk away is trendy Ann Siang Rd, well known for its restored heritage terraces and booty of fashionable restaurants, bars and boutiques. Architecture buffs will appreciate the art deco buildings at Nos 15, 17 and 21. Mosey along it and adjacent Club Street, also famed for its old shophouses, trendy bars, eateries and after-work buzz.

5 Ann Siang Hill Park

At the top of Ann Siang Rd is the entrance to Ann Siang Hill Park. Not only is this Chinatown's highest point, it's a surprising oasis of green in the city centre. Follow the walkways downward to Amoy St.

6 Siang Cho Keong Temple

Small Taoist **Siang Cho Keong Temple** (☎6324 4171; 66 Amoy St; admission free; ◷8am-5pm; MTelok Ayer, Tanjong Pagar) was built by the Hokkien community in 1867–69. Left of the temple entrance you'll see a small 'dragon well': drop a coin and make a wish.

7 Coffee Break

Time for a pit stop at **Coffee Break** (www.facebook.com/coffeebreakamoystreet; 02-78 Amoy Street Food Centre, 7 Maxwell Rd; ◷7.30am-3pm Mon-Fri; MTelok Ayer), a humble drink stall with options like black sesame latte and orange mocha. Make no mistake though, it's still good old Singaporean *kopi* (coffee) – just with a twist.

8 Telok Ayer Street

In Malay, Telok Ayer means 'Water Bay', and Telok Ayer St was a coastal road until land reclamation efforts in the 19th century. Seek out Al-Abrar Mosque, built in the 1850s, Thian Hock Keng Temple, the oldest Hokkien temple in Singapore, and Nagore Durgha Shrine, a mosque built between 1828 and 1830 by Chulia Muslims from South India.

A
B
C
D

1

Pearl's Hill Reservoir

Pearl's Hill City Park

Park Cres

Upper Cross St

6 👁 Ojok Lali

People's Park Complex
👁 7

M Chinatown

Chinatown Heritage Centre 👁

Pagoda St

2

Pearl Bank

Pearl's Hill Tce

Eu Tong Sen St
New Bridge Rd

Temple St

Trengganu St

Smith St

13 ✕

33

34 ☆

Ⓟ 25

Sago St

Singapore Visitor Centre ⓘ @Chinatown

Banda

Buddha Tooth Relic Temple

3

Outram Rd

M Outram Park

Keong Saik Rd

Kreta Ayer Rd

32 ☆

Spring St

South Brid R

CHINATOWN

3

4

Outram Park M

Eu Tong Sen St
New Bridge Rd

Outram Rd

Keong Saik Rd

Teck Lim Rd

Chuan Rd

Bukit Pasoh Rd

✕ 8
Ⓟ 21

28
Ⓟ

✕ 15

30
Ⓟ

Neon Pigeon ✕

Neil Rd

Ⓟ 31

20
Ⓟ

Duxton Hill

Murray St

Maxwell Rd

✕ 12

Murray T

5

Neil Rd

◀ 👁 1
◀ Ⓟ 26

Cantonment Rd

39
🔒

Craig Rd

TANJONG PAGAR

Duxton Rd

Tanjong Pagar Rd

Cook St

Tras St

✕ 14

E

F

G

H

Chulia St

1

0   200 m

0   0.1 miles

South Bridge Rd

Hokien St

Church St

Phillip St

per Cross St

Nankin St

9

Mosque St

Chin Chew St

China St

Pekin St

Market St

Malacca St

2

Republic Plaza

Sri Mariamman Temple

Cross St

17

Amoy St

Telok Ayer St

2

40

Club St

29

23

Telok Ayer

Cecil St

24

37

38

Market St

19

Robinson Rd

Ann Siang Hill

Amoy St

Boon Tat St

Cross St

3

35

Ann Siang Rd

Ann Siang Hill Park

Thian Hock Keng Temple

18

11

10

4

Telok Ayer St

Stanley St

Raffles Quay

Erskine Rd

22

27

Boon Tat St

Kadayanallur St

Cecil St

Robinson Rd

Singapore City Gallery

McCallum St

Maxwell Link

Shenton Way

4

MARINA SOUTH

Maxwell Rd

5

For reviews see

◉	Top Sights	p66
◎	Sights	p72
✕	Eating	p74
🍷	Drinking	p78
★	Entertainment	p81
🔒	Shopping	p83

Sights

Baba House   MUSEUM

1 ◉ Map p70, A5

Baba House is one of Singapore's best-preserved Peranakan heritage homes. Built in the 1890s, it's a wonderful window into the life of an affluent Peranakan family living in Singapore a century ago. Its loving restoration has seen every detail attended to, from the carved motifs on the blue facade down to the door screens. The only way in is on a guided tour, held every Monday, Tuesday, Thursday and Saturday, but the tour is excellent and free. Bookings, by telephone, are essential. (☏ 6227 5731; www.nus.edu.sg/cfa/museum/about.php; 157 Neil Rd; admission free; ⊙ 1hr tours 2pm Mon, 2pm & 6.30pm Tue, 10am Thu, 11am Sat; M Outram Park)

Sri Mariamman Temple   HINDU TEMPLE

2 ◉ Map p70, E2

Paradoxically in the middle of Chinatown, this is the oldest Hindu temple in Singapore, originally built in 1823, then rebuilt in 1843. You can't miss the fabulously animated, Technicolor 1930s *gopuram* (tower) above the entrance, the key to the temple's South Indian Dravidian style. Sacred cow sculptures grace the boundary walls, while the *gopuram* is covered in kitsch plasterwork images of Brahma the creator, Vishnu the preserver and Shiva the destroyer. (☏ 6223 4064; 244

South Bridge Rd; take photos/videos S$3/6; ⊙ 7am-noon & 6-9pm; M Chinatown)

Buddha Tooth Relic Temple   BUDDHIST TEMPLE

3 ◉ Map p70, D3

Consecrated in 2008, this hulking, five-storey Buddhist temple is home to what is reputedly the left canine tooth of the Buddha, recovered from his funeral pyre in Kushinagar, northern India. While its authenticity is debated, the relic enjoys VIP status inside a 420kg solid-gold stupa in a dazzlingly ornate 4th-floor room. More religious relics await at the 3rd-floor Buddhism museum, while the peaceful rooftop garden features a huge prayer wheel inside a 10,000 Buddha Pavilion. (☏ 6220 0220; www.btrts.org.sg; 288 South Bridge Rd; admission free; ⊙ 7am-7pm, relic viewing 9am-6pm; M Chinatown)

Thian Hock Keng Temple   TAOIST TEMPLE

4 ◉ Map p70, F3

Surprisingly, Chinatown's oldest and most important Hokkien temple is often a haven of tranquillity. Built between 1839 and 1842, it's a beautiful place, and once the favourite landing point of Chinese sailors, before land reclamation pushed the sea far down the road. Typically, the temple's design features are richly symbolic: the stone lions at the entrance ward off evil spirits, while the painted depiction of phoenixes and peonies in the central hall symbolise peace and good tidings

Buddha Tooth Relic Temple

respectively. (☎6423 4616; www.thian-hockkeng.com.sg; 158 Telok Ayer St; admission free; ⏱7.30am-5.30pm; Ⓜ Telok Ayer)

Singapore City Gallery   MUSEUM

5 ◉ Map p70, E4

See into Singapore's future at this interactive city-planning exhibition, which provides compelling insight into the government's resolute policies of land reclamation, high-rise housing and meticulous urban planning. The highlight is an 11m-by-11m scale model of the central city, which shows just how different Singapore will look once all the projects currently under development join the skyline. (☎6321 8321; www.ura.gov.sg/citygallery; URA Bldg,

45 Maxwell Rd; admission free; ⏱9am-5pm Mon-Sat; Ⓜ Chinatown, Tanjong Pagar)

Ojok Lali   MASSAGE

6 ◉ Map p70, D1

Tucked away into retro People's Park Centre (not to be confused with neighbouring People's Park Complex), this small, no-frills massage joint specialises in Javanese massage. It's cheap and justifiably popular, so it's always a good idea to call ahead, especially if you're planning on an afternoon rubdown. (☎6341 1875; 02-79 People's Park Centre, 101 Upper Cross St; 1hr body massage S$40; ⏱10am-9pm; Ⓜ Chinatown)

○ Local Life

Pinnacle@Duxton

For killer city views at a bargain, head to the 50th-floor rooftop of **Pinnacle@Duxton** (Map p70, B5; www.pinnacleduxton.com.sg; Block 1G, 1 Cantonment Rd; admission $5; ⊙9am-9pm; Ⓜ Outram Park, Tanjong Pagar). the world's largest public housing complex. Skybridges connecting the seven towers provide a gob-smacking, 360-degree sweep of city, port and sea. Chilling out is encouraged, with patches of lawn, modular furniture and sun lounges. Although a makeshift ticket booth was operating on our last visit, payment is usually by Ez-link transport card only; simply rest your Ez-link card on the ticket machine located at the bottom of Block G to pay.

People's Park Complex MASSAGE

7 ◎ Map p70, C2

Heady with the scent of Tiger balm, Singapore's oldest mall is well known for its cheap massage joints. Our favourite of these is **Mr Lim Foot Reflexology** (☑63274498; 1hr foot reflexology S$25; ⊙10.30am-10pm), where your robust rubdown comes complete with televised local and Taiwanese soaps. If you're feeling adventurous then try one of the fish-pond foot spas, where schools of fish nibble the dead skin right off your feet. (www.peoplesparkcomplex.sg; 1 Park Cres; ⊙9am-10pm, shop times vary; Ⓜ Chinatown)

Eating

Burnt Ends BARBECUE $$$

8 ✕ Map p70, C3

The best seats at this mod-Oz hot spot are at the counter, which offers a prime view of chef Dave Pynt and his 4-tonne, wood-fired ovens and custom grills. The affable Aussie cut his teeth under Spanish charcoal deity Victor Arguinzoniz (Asador Etxebarri), an education echoed in pulled pork shoulder in homemade brioche, and beef marmalade and pickles on chargrilled sourdough.

The produce-driven, sharing-style menu changes daily, while the drinks list showcases smaller wineries and microbreweries. Reservations only taken at noon and 12.30pm for lunch and 6pm and 6.30pm for dinner – book in advance or get here early to add your name to the list. (☑6224 3933; www.burntends.com.sg; 20 Teck Lim Rd; dishes S$8-45; ⊙11.45am-2pm & 6-11pm Wed-Sat, 6-11pm Tue; Ⓜ Chinatown, Outram Park)

Momma Kong's SEAFOOD $$$

9 ✕ Map p70, E2

Small, funky Momma Kong's is run by two young brothers and a cousin obsessed with crab. While the compact menu features numerous finger-licking, MSG-free crab classics, opt for the phenomenal chilli crab, its kick and non-gelatinous gravy unmatched in this town. One serve of crab and four giant, fresh *mantou* (Chinese bread buns) should happily feed two stomachs.

Unlike many other chilli-crab joints, you'll find fixed prices, which means no unpleasant surprises when it's payment time. Book two days ahead (three days for Friday and Saturday) or take a chance and head in late. (☑6225 2722; www.mommakongs.com; 34 Mosque St; crab dishes S\$48, set menu for 2 from S\$126; ⏲5-10pm Mon-Fri, 11am-10pm Sat & Sun; Ⓜ Chinatown)

Ding Dong   SOUTHEAST ASIAN \$\$\$

10 🍴 Map p70, E3

From the graphic bar tiles to the meticulous cocktails to the wow-oh-wow modern takes on Southeast Asian flavours, it's all about attention to detail at this sucker-punch champ. Book a table and drool over zingtastic scallop tartare with fresh coconut, sultry pork ribs with ginger and apricot, or 48-hour beef-cheek *rendang* with wild puffed rice and crispy herbs. (☑6557 0189; www.dingdong.com.sg; 01-02, 115 Amoy St; dishes S\$16-29, 'feed me' menus S\$56-80; ⏲noon-3pm & 6pm-midnight Mon-Fri, 6pm-midnight Sat; Ⓜ Telok Ayer)

Bird Bird   THAI \$\$

11 🍴 Map p70, E3

Banging chicken dishes are the game at this 1960s Bangkok-esque eatery, helmed by chef Bjorn Shen of **Artichoke** (☑6336 6949; www.artichoke.com.sg; 161 Middle Rd; mains S\$18-45; ⏲6.30-9.45pm Tue-Fri, 11.30am-3.30pm & 6.30-9.45pm Sat, 11.30am-3.30pm Sun;

Ⓜ Bugis, Bras Basah) fame. Opt for your bird done Issan barbecue-style or Bangkok fried, the former tender and juicy and the latter super crunchy. Arrive early as there's a no-booking policy; look for the 'palace of Thai chicken' signboard that marks this hot spot. (www.facebook.com/birdbirdsg; 18 Ann Siang Rd; mains S\$10-35; ⏲11.30am-2.30pm Tue-Sat, 6.30-10pm Tue-Thu, 6.30-11pm Fri & Sat; Ⓜ Chinatown, Telok Ayer)

Maxwell Food Centre   HAWKER \$

12 🍴 Map p70, D4

One of Chinatown's most accessible hawker centres, Maxwell is a solid spot to savour some of the city's

---

Q Local Life

Everton Park HBD

The ground-floor space of Singapore's public housing blocks (HDBs) are usually scattered with gossipy uncles and aunties and shrieking kids. At Everton Park, however, you're just as likely to find third wave coffee geeks. The HDB complex is home to **Nylon Coffee Roasters** (Map p70, B5; ☑6220 2330; www.nyloncoffee.sg; 4 Everton Park, 01-40; ⏲8.30am-5.30pm Mon & Wed-Fri, 9am-6pm Sat & Sun; Ⓜ Outram Park, Tanjong Pagar), a standing-room-only cafe-roastery, which also sells a range of design savvy merchandise. Everton Park is 500m south of Outram Park MRT. Enter from Cantonment Rd, directly opposite the seven-tower Pinnacle@Duxton (p74)..

ROSLAN RAHMAN/AFP/GETTY IMAGES ©

Patrons queue for Hong Kong Soya Sauce Chicken Rice & Noodle

street-food staples. While stalls slip in and out of favour with Singapore's fickle diners, enduring favourites include **Tian Tian Hainanese Chicken Rice** (01-10 Maxwell Food Centre, cnr Maxwell & South Bridge Rds; chicken rice from S$3.50; ⊙10am-5pm Tue-Sun; Ⓜ Chinatown) and **Rojak, Popiah & Cockle** (01-56 Maxwell Food Centre, cnr Maxwell & South Bridge Rds; popiah S$2.50, rojak from S$3; ⊙noon-10.30pm; Ⓜ Chinatown). (cnr Maxwell & South Bridge Rds; dishes from S$2.50; ⊙stalls hours vary; ♻; Ⓜ Chinatown)

Chinatown Complex   HAWKER $

13 ✗ Map p70, C2

Leave Smith St's revamped 'Chinatown Food Street' to the out-of-towners and join old-timers and foodies at this nearby labyrinth, now home to Michelin-starred hawker stall **Hong Kong Soya Sauce Chicken Rice & Noodle** (02-126 Chinatown Complex, dishes S$2-3; ⊙10.30am-7pm Mon, Tue, Thu & Fri, from 8.30am Sat & Sun). You decide if the two-hour wait is worth it.

Other standouts include mixed claypot rice at **Lian He Ben Ji Claypot Rice** (☎6227 2470; 02-198/199 Chinatown Complex, dishes S$2.50-20, claypot rice from S$5; ⊙4.30-10pm Fri-Wed) and the rich, nutty satay at **Shi Xiang Satay** (02-79 Chinatown Complex, satay from S$6; ⊙3.30-9pm Fri-Wed). (11 New Bridge Rd; dishes from S$3; ⊙stall hours vary; Ⓜ Chinatown)

Ginza Tendon Itsuki JAPANESE $

14 🍴 Map p70, D5

Life's few certainties include taxes, death and a queue outside this dedicated *tendon* (tempura served on rice) eatery. Patience is rewarded with cries of *irrashaimase!* (welcome) and generous bowls of Japanese comfort grub. Both the tempura and rice are cooked to perfection, drizzled in sweet and sticky soy sauce, and served with *chawanmushi* (Japanese egg custard), miso soup and pickled vegetables. A cash-only bargain. (☎6221 6678; www.tendon-itsuki. sg; 101 Tanjong Pagar Rd; mains S$12.90-13.90; ⏰11.30am-2.30pm & 5.30-10pm; 🍴; ⓂTanjong Pagar)

Meta FRENCH $$$

15 🍴 Map p70, C4

It's all about French food with a delicate Asian twist at this sleek new eatery in trendy Keong Saik Rd. The open kitchen runs nearly the length of this very long and narrow space, with the high stools positioned so guests have front-row seats as chefs create delectable masterpieces. The evolutionary menu changes with the seasons. (☎6513 0898; www.metarestaurant.sg; 9 Keong Saik Rd; set lunch/dinner S$58/118; ⏰noon-2pm Mon-Fri, 5.30pm-midnight Mon-Sat; 🍴; ⓂChinatown, Outram Park)

Ci Yan Organic Vegetarian Health Food VEGETARIAN $

16 🍴 Map p70, E3

Excellent food, a very friendly manager and an informal atmosphere make this a fine choice for a no-fuss vegetarian meal in the heart of Chinatown. It tends to only have five or six dishes (when we ate here choices ranged from the delicious brown-rice set meal to wholemeal hamburgers, vegetarian Penang laksa and almond tofu), written up on a blackboard each day.

Also offers an interesting range of fruit drinks. (☎6225 9026; www.facebook.com/ciyanveg; 8-10 Smith St; mains S$4-8; ⏰noon-10pm; 🍴; ⓂChinatown)

☑ Top Tip

Chope! This seat mine!

Singaporean hawker centres are renowned for not supplying napkins, so it's always best to carry a packet of tissues yourself. Locals also use these to 'chope' their seats during peak periods. The system is simple; just place the tissue packet on the empty seat and ta-dah, no one will sit there. This of course means you shouldn't sit at a 'choped' seat either, unless you wish to feel the wrath of a scorned chopper. Tissue packet sellers are common; S$2 will generally get you a few packets.

Ya Kun Kaya Toast   CAFE $

17 🍴 Map p70, F2

Though it's now part of a chain, this airy, retro coffeeshop is an institution, and the best way to start the day the Singaporean way. The speciality is buttery *kaya* (coconut jam) toast, dipped in runny egg (add black pepper and a few drops of soy sauce) and washed down with strong *kopi*. (📞6438 3638; www.yakun.com; 01-01 Far East Sq, 18 China St; kaya toast set S$4.80; ⏰7.30am-7pm Mon-Fri, to 4.30pm Sat, 8.30am-3pm Sun; Ⓜ Telok Ayer)

Lau Pa Sat   HAWKER $

18 🍴 Map p70, H3

Lau Pa Sat means 'Old Market' in Hokkien, which is appropriate since the handsome iron structure shipped out from Glasgow in 1894 remains intact. The real magic happens on the facing street, when Boon Tat St transforms into **Satay Street** (satay per stick around S$0.60; ⏰7pm-1am Mon-Fri, 3pm-1am Sat & Sun), a KL-style sprawl of tables, beer-peddling aunties and smoky satay stalls. (www.laupasat.biz; 18 Raffles Quay; dishes from S$4, satay from S$0.60; ⏰24hr, individual stalls vary; Ⓜ Telok Ayer, Raffles Place)

Drinking

Operation Dagger   COCKTAIL BAR

19 🍷 Map p70, E3

From the 'cloud-like' light sculpture to the boundary-pushing cocktails, 'extraordinary' is the keyword here.

To encourage experimentation, libations are described by flavour, not spirit, the latter shelved in uniform, apothecary-like bottles. Sample the sesame-infused 'gomashio', or the textural surprise of the 'hot & cold'. Head up the hill where Club Street and Ann Siang Hill meet; a symbol shows the way. (📞6438 4057; www.operationdagger.com; 7 Ann Siang Hill; ⏰6pm-late Tue-Sat; Ⓜ Chinatown, Telok Ayer)

Tippling Club   COCKTAIL BAR

20 🍷 Map p70, D4

Tippling Club propels mixology to dizzying heights, with a technique and creativity that could turn a teetotaller into a born-again soak. The best seats are at the bar, where under a ceiling of hanging bottles, passionate pros turn rare and precious spirits into wonders like the 'smokey old bastard', a mellow concoction of whisky, Peychaud's bitters, cigar and orange. (📞6475 2217; www.tipplingclub.com; 38 Tanjong Pagar Rd; ⏰noon-midnight Mon-Fri, 6pm-midnight Sat; Ⓜ Outram Park, Tanjong Pagar)

Potato Head Folk   COCKTAIL BAR

21 🍷 Map p70, C4

Offshoot of the legendary Bali bar, this standout, multi-level playground incorporates three spaces, all reached via a chequered stairwell pimped with creepy storybook murals and giant glowing dolls. Skip the Three Buns burger joint and head straight for the dark, plush glamour of cocktail lounge Studio 1939 or the laid-back frivolity of the rooftop tiki bar. (📞6327 1939;

www.pttheadfolk.com; 36 Keong Saik Rd;
⏱Studio 1939 & rooftop bar 5pm-midnight
Tue-Sun; 🛜; Ⓜ Outram Park)

Spiffy Dapper
COCKTAIL BAR

22 🚇 Map p70, F4

Keep your eyes peeled for the Dapper
Coffee sign and then quick, before
anyone sees, scuttle up the stairs and
through the engraved doors. Choose
from the list of classic cocktails or let
the bar tenders do their thing – gin
lovers you're in for a treat as the collection here is legendary. (📞8233 9810;
www.spiffydapper.com; 73 Amoy St; ⏱5pm
till late Mon-Fri, from 6pm Sat & Sun; Ⓜ Telok
Ayer)

Bitters & Love
COCKTAIL BAR

23 🚇 Map p70, G3

Look for the bottle-shaped lights,
swing open the door and dive into
this affable, oft-damn-loud cocktail
den, home to some of the city's top
barkeeps. Forget the drinks list.
Simply rattle off your mood, favourite
flavours or spirit base and let the
team work their magic. For something local, request a rum-based,
tea-infused Kaya Toast. (📞6438 1836;
www.bittersandlove.com; 118 Telok Ayer St;
⏱6pm-midnight Mon-Thu, to 2am Fri & Sat;
Ⓜ Telok Ayer)

Black Swan
BAR

24 🚇 Map p70, H2

Was that Rita Hayworth? This art deco
marvel is set inside a 1930s bank build-

Local Life
Beer Hawkers

Clink craft beer glasses with locals
at the Chinatown Complex (p76),
where a few fancy beer hawkers
such as Smith Street Taps have
opened their shutters right next
to some of the best eats in town.
Don't be put off if the centre looks
closed when you enter; check the
map at the top of the escalator to
find the stalls, and join the party.

ing. Hit the bustling ground-floor bar
for happy hour oysters (S$2) served
with Stella Artois and house wines
(S$11) from 5pm to 8pm weekdays,
or channel Bette Davis in the Powder
Room, a decadent cocktail lounge.
(📞6438 3757; www.theblackswan.com.sg; 19
Cecil St; ⏱Black Swan 11.30am-11pm Mon,
to midnight Tue-Thu, to 1am Fri & Sat; Powder
Room 5pm-midnight Tue-Thu, to 1am Fri & Sat;
🛜; Ⓜ Raffles Place, Telok Ayer)

Smith Street Taps
BEER STALL

25 🚇 Map p70, D3

Head to this hawker-centre stall for a
top selection of ever-changing craft and
premium draught beers from around
the world. A few food stalls stay open
around this back section of the hawkers
market, creating a local hidden-bar
buzz. (📞9430 2750; www.facebook.com/
smithstreettaps; 02-62 Chinatown Complex,
11 New Bridge Rd; ⏱6.30-10.30pm Tue-Sat;
Ⓜ Chinatown)

Strangers' Reunion CAFE

26 Map p70, A5

A cafe run by Singapore's three-time (and counting) barista champion Ryan Tan equals silky smooth lattes every time you visit. The food (mains S$10.50 to S$27.90), a selection of salads and hearty mains look inviting, but it is the buttermilk waffles that almost threaten to take away the limelight from the coffee. (✆6222 4869; www.facebook.com/StrangersReunion; 33-35 Kampong Bahru Rd; ⊙9am-10pm Sun-Thu, to midnight Fri & Sat; Ⓜ Outram Park)

Kyō CLUB

27 Map p70, G3

From boring bank to pulsating hot spot, this sprawling, Japanese-inspired playpen is home to Singapore's longest bar (expect the odd bar-top booty shake), suited eye-candy, and sharp DJs spinning credible electro, house, funk or disco. If you're itching for a little midweek hedonism, you know where to go. (✆8299 8735; www.clubkyo.com; B2-01 Keck Seng Tower, 133 Cecil St; ⊙10pm-3am Wed & Thu, to 3.30am Fri, to 4.30am Sat; Ⓜ Telok Ayer, Raffles Place)

Tantric Bar BAR, LGBT

28 Map p70, C4

Two indoor bars and two alfresco palm-fringed courtyards is what you get at Singapore's best-loved gay drinking hole. Especially heaving on Friday and Saturday nights, it's a hit with preened locals and eager expats and out-of-towners, who schmooze and cruise to Kylie, Gaga and Katy Perry chart toppers. (✆6423 9232; www.homeofthebluespin.com; 78 Neil Rd; ⊙8pm-3am Sun-Fri, 8pm-4am Sat; Ⓜ Outram Park, Chinatown)

Ô Batignolles WINE BAR

29 Map p70, F2

Don those Breton strips and retreat to this corner bistro for a little joie de vivre. Run by a French couple and never short of unwinding lawyers and hopeless Francophiles, it's a fine choice for a well-priced glass (or bottle) of boutique wine; an *assiette de charcuterie* (selection of cold cuts); and a little Club Steet people watching. (✆6438 3913; www.obatignolles.com; 2 Gemmill Lane; ⊙noon-midnight Mon-Fri, 11am-midnight Sat, 11am-9pm Sun; ; Ⓜ Telok Ayer)

Taboo CLUB, LGBT

30 Map p70, C4

Conquer the dance floor at what remains the favourite gay club in town. Expect the requisite line-up of shirtless gyrators, doting straight women and regular racy themed nights. Note: only the chill-out lounge is open on Wednesday and Thursday nights. (✆6225 6256; www.taboo.sg; 65 Neil Rd; ⊙8pm-2am Wed & Thu, 10pm-3am Fri, 10pm-4am Sat; Ⓜ Outram Park, Chinatown)

Night market on Trengganu Street, Chinatown

Tea Chapter   TEAHOUSE

31  Map p70, D4

Queen Elizabeth and Prince Philip dropped by this tranquil teahouse in 1989, and for S$10 you can sit at the table they sipped at. A minimum charge of S$8 per person will get you a heavenly pot of loose-leaf tea, prepared with traditional precision. The selection is excellent and the adjoining shop sells tea and a selection of beautiful tea sets. (☎6226 1175; www.teachapter.com; 9-11 Neil Rd; ☺teahouse 11am-10.30pm Sun-Thu, to 11pm Fri & Sat, shop 10.30am-10.30pm daily; Ⓜ Chinatown)

Entertainment

Kreta Ayer
People's Theatre   OPERA

32 Map p70, C3

Located just behind People's Park Complex, the Kreta Ayer People's Theatre is well known for staging dramatic Chinese operas. You may not understand a word of what is going on, but it is a wonderful experience. Check the website for current performances. (☎6222 3972; www.kapt.com.sg; 30A Kreta Ayer Rd; Ⓜ Chinatown)

RICHARD I'ANSON/GETTY IMAGES ©

Performer at the Chinese Theatre Circle

Toy Factory Productions THEATRE

33 ⭐ Map p70, D3

Originally focused on puppetry, this bilingual (English and Mandarin) theatre company is now best known for its intercultural collaborations and envelope-pushing local work, performed in various venues across town. Past productions have included a play about Singapore's most famous transsexual and a wicked satire about Singaporean men called *The Penis Society*. Singapore, sterile? Ha! Check the website for details on performances. (☎6222 1526; www.toyfactory.com.sg; 15A Smith St; ⏱9am-6pm; ⓂChinatown)

Chinese Theatre Circle OPERA

34 ⭐ Map p70, D3

Teahouse evenings organised by this nonprofit opera company are a wonderful, informal introduction to Chinese opera. Every Friday and Saturday at 8pm there is a brief talk on Chinese opera, followed by a 45-minute excerpt from an opera classic, performed by actors in full costume. You can also opt for a pre-show Chinese meal at 7pm. Book ahead. (☎6323 4862; www.ctcopera.com; 5 Smith St; show & snacks S$25, show & dinner S$40; ⏱7-9pm Fri & Sat; ⓂChinatown)

Screening Room CINEMA

35 ⭐ Map p70, E3

If your idea of a good night involves sinking into a sofa and watching classic flicks, make some time for Screening Room. Expect anything from *On the Town* to *Sex, Lies and Videotape*, projected onto a pull-down screen. Best of all, people who purchase S$15++ of drinks or food at the cinema's Theatre Bar can watch for free. (☎6221 1694; www.screeningroom.com.sg; 12 Ann Siang Rd; ⊙nightly Mon-Sat; Ⓜ Chinatown, Telok Ayer)

Shopping

Utterly Art ART

36 🔒 Map p70, E2

Climb the stairs to this tiny, welcoming gallery for works by contemporary Singaporean, Filipino and, on occasion, Cambodian artists. While painting is the gallery's focus, exhibitions dabble in sculpture and ceramics on occasion, with artworks priced from around S$500 (depending on the exhibition). Opening times can be a little erratic, so always call ahead if making a special trip. (☎9487 2006; www.utterlyart.com.sg; Level 3, 20B Mosque St; ⊙2-8pm Mon-Sat, noon-5.30pm Sun; Ⓜ Chinatown)

Eu Yan Sang CHINESE MEDICINE

37 🔒 Map p70, E3

Get your *qi* back in order at Singapore's most famous and user-friendly Chinese-medicine store. Pick up some Monkey Bezoar powder to relieve excess phlegm, or Liu Jun Zi pills to dispel dampness. You'll find herbal teas, soups and oils, and you can even consult a practitioner of Chinese medicine at the clinic next door (bring your passport). (☎6223 6333; www.euyansang.com.sg; 269 South Bridge Rd; ⊙shop 10am-10pm, clinic 8.30am-7.30pm Mon-Sat; Ⓜ Chinatown)

Understand

Temple Tales

Before construction of the Thian Hock Keng Temple (p72), the site was home to a much humbler joss house, where Chinese migrants would come to thank Mazu, the goddess of the sea, for their safe arrival. Their donations helped propel construction of the current temple, the low granite barrier of which once served to keep seawater out during high tide. Look up at the temple's ceiling in the right wing and you'll notice a statue of a man, seemingly lifting a beam. The statue is an ode to Indian migrants from nearby Chulia St, who helped construct the building. During restoration works in 1998, one of the roof beams revealed a surprising find – a scroll written by the Qing emperor Guangxu bestowing blessings on Singapore's Chinese community.

Understand

Peranakan Culture

Peranakan heritage has been enjoying renewed interest, mainly triggered by *The Little Nonya*, a high-rating 2008 drama series focused on a Peranakan family, and the opening of Singapore's outstanding Peranakan Museum (p32). But who are the Peranakans?

Origins

In Singapore, Peranakan (locally born) people are the descendants of immigrants who married local, mostly Malay women. The largest Peranakan group in Singapore is the Straits Chinese. The men, called Babas, and the women, Nonya, primarily speak a patois that mixes Bahasa Malaysia, Hokkien dialect and English. The ancestors of the Straits Chinese were mainly traders from mainland China, their presence on the Malay peninsula stretching back to the Ming dynasty. The ancestors of Chitty Melaka and Jawi Peranakan were Indian traders, whose unions with local Malay women created their own unique traditions. All three groups are defined by an intriguing, hybrid culture created by centuries of cultural exchange and adaptation.

Weddings

No Peranakan tradition matches the scale of the traditional wedding. Originally spanning 12 days, its fusion of Fujian Chinese and Malay traditions included the consulting of a *sinseh pokwa* (astrologer) in the choosing of an auspicious wedding day, elaborate gifts delivered to the bride's parents in *bakul siah* (lacquered bamboo containers) and a young boy rolling across the bed three times in the hope for a male first-born. With the groom in Qing-dynasty scholar garb and the bride in a similarly embroidered gown and hat piece, the first day would include a tea ceremony. On the second day, the couple took their first meal together, feeding each other 12 dishes to symbolise the 12-day process, while the third day would see them offering tea to their parents and in-laws. On the *dua belah hari* (12th-day ceremony), the marriage was sealed and proof of the consummation confirmed with a discreet sighting of the stain on the bride's virginity handkerchief by the bride's parents and groom's mother.

Willow and Huxley
FASHION & ACCESSORIES

38 🔒 Map p70, F3

Willow and Huxley offers a sharp, vibrant edit of smaller, independent labels like Australia's Finders Keepers and Bec & Bridge and Denmark's quirky Baum und Pferdgarten. Its range of jewellery spans vintage to statement, with a small selection of casual, beach-friendly threads for men courtesy of Australia's The Critical Slide Society and New York's Onia and Psycho Bunny. (📞6220 1745; www.willowandhuxley.com; 20 Amoy St; ⊙9am-8pm Mon-Fri, 11am-3pm Sat; Ⓜ Telok Ayer)

Tong Mern Sern Antiques
ANTIQUES

39 🔒 Map p70, C5

An Aladdin's cave of dusty furniture, books, records, wood carvings, porcelain and other bits and bobs (we even found an old cash register), Tong Mern Sern is a curious hunting ground for Singapore nostalgia. A banner hung above the front door proclaims: 'We buy junk and sell antiques. Some fools buy. Some fools sell'. Better have your wits about you. (📞6223 1037; 51 Craig St; ⊙9am-6pm Mon-Sat, 1-6pm Sun; Ⓜ Outram Park)

Local Life
Paper, Death & Sago Lane

The curious paper objects on sale around Chinatown – from miniature cars to computers – are offerings burned at funeral wakes to ensure the material wealth of the dead. Veteran **Nam's Supplies** (Map p70, D3; 📞6324 5872; www.nam-supplies.com; 22 Smith St; ⊙8am-7pm; Ⓜ Chinatown) has been peddling such offerings since 1948, when nearby Sago Lane heaved with so-called 'death houses', where dying relatives were sent to spend their final days.

Yong Gallery
ANTIQUES

40 🔒 Map p70, E3

The owner is a calligrapher, and much of his artwork is on sale. You'll also find jewellery, genuine jade products and antiques, as well as more affordable gifts like decorative bookmarks, Chinese fans and clocks. The shop is stuffed with goodies so it's fun browsing even if you're not in a buying mood. (📞6226 1718; www.yonggallery.com; 260 South Bridge Rd; ⊙10am-7pm; Ⓜ Chinatown)

Local Life
Katong (Joo Chiat)

Getting There

Ⓜ MRT Paya Lebar and Eunos stations are the closest stations.

🚍 Bus Routes 33 and 16 service Joo Chiat Rd.

Also known as Joo Chiat, Katong is the heart of Singapore's Peranakan community. It's an evocative mix of multicoloured shophouses, tucked-away temples and quaint workshops and handicraft studios, not to mention some of the city's best eateries. Try to head in during business hours, when locals hop in and out of heirloom shops in search of fabrics, produce and the next tasty snack.

❶ Geylang Serai Market

Geylang Serai Market (1 Geylang Serai; ⊙8am-10pm, individual stalls vary; Ⓜ Paya Lebar) packs in a lively wet market, hawker food centre and stalls selling everything from Malay CDs to skull-caps. Feeling peckish? Hunt down some *pisang goreng* (banana fritters) and wash them down with *bandung* (milk with rose cordial syrup).

❷ Joo Chiat Road

Eclectic Joo Chiat Rd is lined with dusty antiques workshops, Islamic fashion boutiques and low-fuss grocery shops. Detour left into Joo Chiat Tce to admire the Peranakan terraces at Nos 89 to 129, adorned with *pintu pagar* (swinging doors) and colourful ceramic tiles.

❸ Long Phung

Head back to Joo Chiat Rd and continue south to **Long Phung** (📞6440 6959; www.longphungvietrest.com; 159 Joo Chiat Rd; dishes S$7-23; ⊙noon-10pm; 🚍16, 33, Ⓜ Paya Lebar), a down-to-earth Vietnamese eatery serving up Singapore's best Vietnamese food. The *pho* (Vietnamese noodle soup) is gorgeous.

❹ Kuan Im Tng Temple

Fingers licked, it's a quick walk to **Kuan Im Tng Temple** (📞6348 0967; www.kuanimtng.org.sg; cnr Tembeling Rd & Joo Chiat Lane; ⊙5am-6.15pm; 🚍16, 33, Ⓜ Paya Lebar), a Buddhist temple dedicated to Kuan Yin, goddess of mercy. Temple fans will appreciate the ornate roof ridges adorned with dancing dragons.

❺ Koon Seng Road Terraces

Koon Seng Rd is famous for its two rows of prewar, pastel-coloured Peranakan terraces, lavished with stucco dragons, birds, crabs and brilliant glazed tiles imported from Europe.

❻ Sri Senpaga Vinayagar Temple

One of Singapore's most beautiful Hindu temples, **Sri Senpaga Vinayagar Temple** (📞6345 8176; www.senpaga.org.sg; 19 Ceylon Rd; admission free; ⊙6.15am-noon & 6.30-9pm; 🚍10, 12, 14, 32) features a *kamalapaatham*, a specially sculptured granite foot-stone found in certain ancient Hindu temples. The roof of the inner sanctum is covered in gold.

❼ Kim Choo Kueh Chang

Katong is stuffed with bakeries and dessert shops, but few equal old-school **Kim Choo Kueh Chang** (www.kimchoo.com; 109 East Coast Rd; ⊙9am-8.30pm; 🚍10, 14, 16, 32). Pick up traditional pineapple tarts and other Peranakan *kueh* (bite-sized snacks), and pit stop at the adjoining boutique for Peranakan ceramics and clothing.

❽ Katong Antique House

Tiny shop-cum-museum **Katong Antique House** (📞6345 8544; 208 East Coast Rd; 🚍10, 12, 14, 32, 40) is the domain of Peter Wee, a noted expert on Peranakan culture, and packed with his collection of books, antiques and cultural artefacts. By appointment only, though it's sometimes open to the public.

Local Life
Geylang

Getting There

🚌 **Bus** Routes 2, 13, 21, 26 and 51 run along Sims Ave through Geylang.

Ⓜ **MRT** Kallang, Aljunied and Paya Lebar are the closest stations.

Contradiction thrives in Geylang, a neighbourhood as famous for its shrines, temples and mosques as for its brothels and back-alley gambling dens. Head in for lunch, spend the afternoon wandering quaint *lorongs* (alleys), religious buildings and an under-the-radar gallery, then head back to neon-lit Geylang Rd for a long, lively evening of people-watching and unforgettably good local grub.

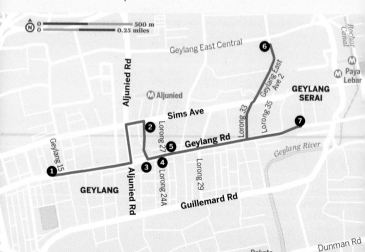

1 Geylang Lor 9 Fresh Frog Porridge

Geylang is famous for its frog porridge and the best place to try it is **Geylang Lor 9 Fresh Frog Porridge** (235 Geylang Rd; frog porridge from S$8.50; ⏰11.45am-3.45am; 🚌2, 51, Ⓜ Kallang). Its Cantonese-style version is beautifully smooth and gooey, and only live frogs are used, so the meat is always fresh.

2 Amitabha Buddhist Centre

Take a class on dharma and meditation at the **Amitabha Buddhist Centre** (📞6745 8547; www.fpmtabc.org; 44 Lorong 25A; ⏰10.30am-6pm Tue-Sat, 10am-6pm Sun; Ⓜ Aljunied); its upstairs meditation hall is open to the public and filled with devotional objects. Check the website for class schedules.

3 No Signboard Seafood

If you didn't brave the frog porridge, get messy over white-pepper crab at **No Signboard Seafood** (📞6842 3415; www.nosignboardseafood.com; 414 Geylang Rd; dishes from S$15-60, crab per kg around S$80; ⏰11am-1am; Ⓜ Aljunied). Madam Ong Kim Hoi started out with an unnamed hawker stall (hence 'No Signboard'), but the popularity of her seafood made her a rich woman, with four restaurants.

4 Lorong 24A

One alley worth strolling down is Lorong 24A, lined with renovated shophouses from which the sounds of chanting emerge. Many have been taken over by the numerous small Buddhist associations in the area.

Close by, tree-lined Lorong 27 is jammed with colourful shrines and temples.

5 Geylang Thian Huat Siang Joss Paper

Old-school **Geylang Thian Huat Siang Joss Paper** (503 Geylang Rd; ⏰8am-9.30pm; Ⓜ Aljunied) sells paper offerings used at funeral wakes. You'll find everything from giant cash registers to lifelike shoes and piles of cash, all thrown into the fire to ensure a comfortable afterlife.

6 Sri Sivan Temple

Built on Orchard Rd in the 1850s, the whimsically ornate **Sri Sivan Temple** (📞6743 4566; www.sstsingapore.com; 24 Geylang East Ave 2; admission free; ⏰6am-noon & 6-9pm; Ⓜ Paya Lebar) was uprooted and moved to Serangoon Rd in the 1980s before moving to its current location in 1993. The Hindu temple is unique for its fusion of North and South Indian architectural influences.

7 Rochor Beancurd

End on a sweet note at tiny **Rochor Beancurd** (📞6748 3989; www.rochorbeancurdhouse.wix.com/home; 745 Geylang Rd; dough sticks S$1.10, bean curd from S$1.50; ⏰24hr; ✏; Ⓜ Paya Lebar). People head here from all over the city for a bowl of silky bean curd (opt for it warm). Order a side of dough sticks and dip to your heart's content. Oh, and did we mention the egg tarts?

Local Life
Changi & Pulau Ubin

Getting There

🚌 **Bus** No 2 from Tanah Merah MRT reaches Changi Village. Bumboats (one way S$3, bicycle surcharge S$2; 6am to 9pm) connect Changi Village to Pulau Ubin.

Singapore's 'Far East' serves up a slower, nostalgic style of local life. Vests, boardshorts and flip-flops are the look in chilled-out Changi Village, a place where low-rise buildings are the norm and out-of-towners are a less common sight. A short bumboat (motorised sampan) ride away, the rustic island of Pulau Ubin is the Singapore that development has mercifully left behind... for now.

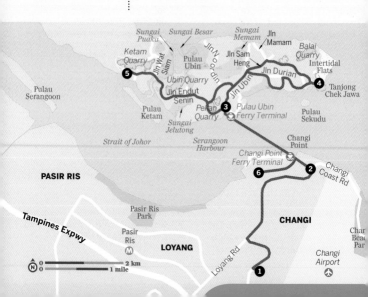

❶ Changi Museum & Chapel

Although no longer at the original Changi prison site, the **Changi Museum & Chapel** (☎6214 2451; www.changimuseum.sg; 1000 Upper Changi Rd N; audioguide adult/child S$8/4; ⏰9.30am-5pm, last entry 4.30pm; Ⓜ Tanah Merah, then bus 2) remains a moving tribute to the Allied POWs captured, imprisoned and subjected to horrific treatment by the invading Japanese forces during WWII. Its centrepiece is a replica of the original Changi Chapel built by inmates.

❷ Changi Village

Hugging Singapore's far northeast coast, Changi Village is well worth a wander to experience a curiously relaxed side of Singapore. The vibe is almost village-like, and a browse around the area will turn up cheap clothes, batik, Indian textiles and electronics. Bumboats to Pulau Ubin depart from Changi Point Ferry Terminal, beside the bus terminal.

❸ Pulau Ubin Village

Your landing spot on Pulau Ubin is Pulau Ubin Village. Although not technically a tourist sight, its ramshackle nature channels a long-lost Singapore. If you're feeling peckish, turn left for a handful of eateries, mostly housed in *kampong* (village) huts. Tuck into noodles, rice dishes or seafood staples like chilli crab (expect to pay around S$25 per person for the latter). The village is also the place to rent bikes; day rentals cost around S$5 to S$12.

❹ Chek Jawa Wetlands

If you only have time for one part of Pulau Ubin, make it **Chek Jawa Wetlands** (admission free; ⏰8.30am-6pm). Located at the island's eastern end, its 1km coastal boardwalk juts out into the sea before looping back through protected mangrove swamp to the 20m-high Jejawi Tower, offering a stunning panorama. You can't bring your bike into the reserve so make sure you rent one that comes with a bike lock.

❺ German Girl Shrine

Housed in a brand-new hardwood hut, the German Girl Shrine is one of the island's quirkier sights. Legend has it that the young German daughter of a coffee plantation manager was running away from British troops who had come to arrest her parents during WWI and fell fatally into the quarry behind her house. Somewhere along the way, this daughter of a Roman Catholic family became a Taoist deity, whose help some Chinese believers seek for good health and fortune.

❻ Coastal Settlement

Back in Changi, end the day with drinks at **Coastal Settlement** (☎6475 0200; www.thecoastalsettlement.com; 200 Netheravon Rd; ⏰10.30am-midnight Tue-Sun, last orders 9.30pm; Ⓜ Tampines, then bus 29), an eclectic bar-lounge-restaurant pimped with retro objects and set in a black-and-white colonial bungalow on lush, verdant grounds.

Explore

Little India & Kampong Glam

Little India bursts with vibrancy. This is a world where goods crowd the five-foot-ways, shophouses are the colour of crayons (see above) and men in *dhotis* (loincloths) gossip over authentic *dosa* (savoury pancakes) at the marketplace. Walk 15 minutes southeast and you're in calmer Kampong Glam, dubbed Arab St. Head here for beautiful mosques, vibrant fabrics, trendy boutiques and delicious grub.

The Sights in a Day

🔅 Breakfast South Indian style at **Ananda Bhavan** (p106), explore the lively market stalls of **Tekka Centre** (p95) and drop into Hindu showpiece **Sri Veeramakaliamman Temple** (p98). To learn more about the rich history of Singapore's Indian community, spend an hour or so exploring the impressive, multimedia **Indian Heritage Centre** (p98).

☀️ Recharge with Indian home-cooking at **Lagnaa Barefoot Dining** (p103), seek good fortune at the reputedly lucky **Kuan Im Thong Hood Cho Temple** (p101), then try your luck scoring a bargain at **Bugis Street Market** (p113). Next stop: Kampong Glam. If you're not shopped out, pick up a bespoke fragrance at **Sifr Aromatics** (p110) and local design at **Supermama** (p110). Alternatively, head straight to heritage **Sultan Mosque** (p99).

🌙 Come dinner, opt for Mexican, margaritas and people watching at **Piedra Negra** (p105), real-deal Italian at **Cicheti** (p103) or dirt-cheap *murtabak* (stuffed savoury pancake) at no-frills **Zam Zam** (p103). Cap it off with made-to-measure cocktails at **Maison Ikkoku** (p107) or live tunes at **BluJaz Café** (p109) or **Going Om** (p109).

For a local's day in Little India, see p94.

🔍 **Local Life**

A Stroll in Little India (p94)

💜 **Best of Singapore**

Food
Kilo (p102)

Lagnaa Barefoot Dining (p103)

Zam Zam (p103)

Drinking
Maison Ikkoku (p107)

Beast (p107)

Artistry (p107)

Druggists (p107)

Shopping
Sifr Aromatics (p110)

Supermama (p110)

Haji Lane (p113)

Getting There

Ⓜ **MRT** Little India (Purple Line) station is right by the Tekka Centre. You can also walk here from Rochor (Blue Line), Bugis (Blue and Green Lines) and Farrer Park (Purple Line) stations. Bugis is best for Kampong Glam, and Jalan Besar is easily reached from Lavender (Green Line) or Farrer Park.

Local Life
A Stroll in Little India

Loud, colourful and refreshingly raffish, Little India stands in contrast to the more sanitised parts of the city. Dive into a gritty, pungent wonderland of dusty grocery shops, gold and sari traders, haggling Indian families and heady Hindu temples. Jumble them all together with a gut-busting booty of fiery eateries and you have Singapore's most hypnotic, electrifying urban experience.

1 Buffalo Road

Plunge into subcontinental Singapore on Buffalo Rd. It's a bustling strip packed with brightly coloured facades, Indian produce shops, Hindu shrines and garland stalls. Flowers used to make the garlands are highly symbolic: both the lotus and the white jasmine spell purity, while the yellow marigold denotes peace.

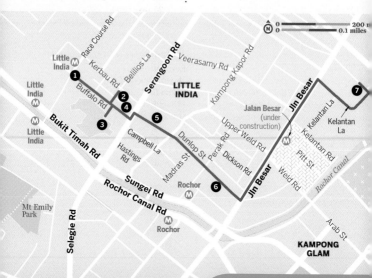

❷ Tan House

As you walk up Buffalo Rd towards Serangoon Rd, look for an alley leading to Kerbau Rd on your left. Take a quick detour down it to be dazzled by Tan House. Sitting on the corner of the alley and Kerbau Rd, this is quite possibly Singapore's most colourful building. Once you're Instagrammed out, head back onto Buffalo Rd.

❸ Tekka Centre Wet Market

If it's morning, scour the wet market inside **Tekka Centre** (Map p96, A5; cnr Serangoon & Buffalo Rds; dishes S\$3-10; ◷7am-11pm; ✈; Ⓜ Little India), where locals battle it out for the city's freshest produce. It's an intense place, stocking everything from fresh yoghurt and dried curry spices to bitter gourds, black-skin chicken and halal meats. If you're after a sari, the top floor has a swarm of vendors.

❹ Nalli

For quality cotton and silk saris, many locals head to **Nalli** (☎6299 3949; www.nallisingapore.com.sg; 10 Buffalo Rd; ◷10am-9pm; Ⓜ Little India) directly opposite the Tekka Centre. It's a small, industrious shop where you can pick up cotton saris for as little as S\$30. If money isn't an issue, consider opting for one of the beautiful silk versions, most of which are upstairs. These usually go for between S\$100 and S\$1000.

❺ Thandapani Co

Slip into Dunlop St and look for **Thandapani Co** (124 Dunlop St; ◷9.30am-9.30pm; Ⓜ Little India). Adorned with hessian bags packed with chillies, fennel seeds and other Indian staples, this grocery shop is considered one of the city's best spice vendors, stocking ingredients you won't find elsewhere.

❻ Abdul Gafoor Mosque

Equally enticing is **Abdul Gafoor Mosque** (☎6295 4209; 41 Dunlop St; admission free; ◷8am-8pm Sat-Thu, 8amnoon & 2.30-8pm Fri; Ⓜ Rochor, Little India), with its peculiar mix of Islamic and Victorian architecture. Completed in 1910, it features an elaborate sundial crowning its main entrance, each of its 25 rays decorated with Arabic calligraphy denoting the names of 25 prophets.

❼ Sungei Road Laksa

End your local adventure with a cheap, steamy fix at **Sungei Road Laksa** (01-100, Block 27, Jln Berseh; laksa S\$3; ◷9am-5pm, closed 1st & 3rd Wed of month; Ⓜ Rochor). The fragrant, savoury, coconut-base soup enjoys a cult following, and only charcoal is used to keep the precious gravy warm. To avoid the lunchtime crowds, head in before 11.30am or after 2pm.

Lavender St

Foch Rd

Tyrwhitt Rd

Horne Rd

Jln Besar Stadium

King George's Ave

Twin Rd

Sturdee Rd

Jln Besar

Petain Rd

Plumer Rd

Kitchener Rd

Townshend Rd

Beatty Rd

Sri Vadapathira 4
Kaliamman
Temple

Serangoon Rd

Maude Rd

Race Course Rd

Sri Srinivasa
Perumal
Temple 5

Kitchener Rd

Sam Leong Rd

Verdun Rd

Tessensohn Rd

Syed Alwi Rd

Serangoon
Plaza

47

Kampong Kapor Rd

Owen Rd

Desker Rd

Rowell Rd

LITTLE INDIA

Rangoon Rd

Farrer
Park

Burmah Rd

Birch Rd

Babboo La

Hindoo La

Norris Rd

20

Owen Rd

Roberts La

Kinta Rd

Race Course La

Klang La

Serangoon Rd

Veerasamy Rd

Sri
Veeramakaliamman
Temple 3

Northumberland Rd

Race Course Rd

Chander Rd

400 m
0.25 miles

For reviews see	
⊙ Sights	p98
⊗ Eating	p102
⊗ Drinking	p107
⊙ Entertainment	p109
⊞ Shopping	p110

Farrer
Park
Fields

Hampshire Rd

Little
India

Kerbau Rd

Sights

Indian Heritage Centre   MUSEUM

1 ◎ Map p96, B5

Delve into the heritage of Singapore's Indian community at this showpiece museum. Divided into five themes, its hundreds of historical and cultural artefacts explore everything from early interactions between South Asia and Southeast Asia to Indian cultural traditions and the contributions of Indian Singaporeans to the development of the island nation. Among the more extraordinary objects is a 19th-century Chettinad doorway, intricately adorned with 5000 minute carvings. (☑6291 1601; www.indianheritage.org.sg; 5 Campbell Lane; adult/child under 7yr S$4/free; ◎10am-7pm Tue-Thu, to 8pm Fri & Sat, to 4pm Sun; Ⓜ Little India, Rochor)

Little India Arcade   MARKET

2 ◎ Map p96, A5

This modest but colourful area of wall-to-wall shops, pungent aromas and Hindi film music is a welcome contrast to the prim modernity of many parts of the city. The arcade has an inside section as well as shops running along Campbell Lane. It's the place to come to pick up that framed print of Krishna you've always wanted, eat great food and watch street-side cooks fry chapatis. (☑6295 5998; www.littleindiaarcade.com.sg; 48 Serangoon Rd; ◎9am-10pm; Ⓜ Little India)

Sri Veeramakaliamman Temple   HINDU TEMPLE

3 ◎ Map p96, B4

Little India's most colourful, visually stunning temple is dedicated to the ferocious goddess Kali, depicted wearing a garland of skulls, ripping out the insides of her victims, and sharing more tranquil family moments with her sons Ganesh and Murugan. The bloodthirsty consort of Shiva has always been popular in Bengal, the birthplace of the labourers who built the structure in 1881. The temple is at its most evocative during each of the four daily *puja* (prayer) sessions. (☑6295 4538; www.sriveeramakaliamman.com; 141 Serangoon Rd; admission free; ◎8am-noon & 6.30-9pm Mon-Thu & Sat, 8am-noon & 6-9pm Fri & Sun; Ⓜ Little India)

Sri Vadapathira Kaliamman Temple   HINDU TEMPLE

4 ◎ Map p96, D1

Dedicated to Kaliamman, the Destroyer of Evil, this South Indian temple began life in 1870 as a modest shrine but underwent a significant facelift in 1969 to transform it into the beauty standing today. The carvings here – particularly on the *vimana* (domed structure within the temple) – are among the best temple artwork you'll see anywhere in Singapore. (☑6298 5053; www.srivadapathirakali.org; 555 Serangoon Rd; admission free; ◎6am-noon & 4.30-9pm Sun-Thu, 6am-12.30pm & 4.30-9.30pm Fri & Sat; Ⓜ Farrer Park, Boon Keng)

KIMBERLEY COOLE/GETTY IMAGES ©

Hindu deity at Sri Veeramakaliamman Temple

Sri Srinivasa Perumal Temple

HINDU TEMPLE

5 ⊙ Map p96, C2

Dedicated to Vishnu, this temple dates from 1855, but the striking, 20m-tall *gopuram* (tower) is a S$300,000 1966 add-on. Inside is a statue of Vishnu, his sidekicks Lakshmi and Andal, and his bird-mount Garuda. The temple is the starting point for a colourful, wince-inducing street parade during the Thaipusam festival: to show their devotion, many participants pierce their bodies with hooks and skewers. (☑6298 5771; https://heb.org.sg; 397 Serangoon Rd; admission free; ⊙6.30am-noon & 6-9pm; Ⓜ Farrer Park)

Sultan Mosque

MOSQUE

6 ⊙ Map p96, E7

Seemingly pulled from the pages of the *Arabian Nights,* Singapore's largest mosque is nothing short of enchanting, designed in the Saracenic style and topped by a golden dome. It was originally built in 1825 with the aid of a grant from Raffles and the East India Company, after Raffles' treaty with the sultan of Singapore allowed the Malay leader to retain sovereignty over the area. In 1928, the original mosque was replaced by the present magnificent building, designed by an Irish architect. (☑6293 4405; www.sultanmosque.org.sg; 3 Muscat St; admission free; ⊙9.30am-noon & 2-4pm Sat-Thu, 2.30-4pm Fri; Ⓜ Bugis)

Malay Heritage Centre   MUSEUM

7 🎯 Map p96, E7

The Kampong Glam area is the historic seat of Malay royalty, resident here before the arrival of Raffles, and the *istana* (palace) on this site was built for the last sultan of Singapore, Ali Iskander Shah, between 1836 and 1843. It's now a museum, its recently revamped galleries exploring Malay-Singaporean culture and history, from the early migration of traders to Kampong Glam to the development of Malay-Singaporean film, theatre, music and publishing. (☎6391 0450; www.malayheritage.org.sg;

Local Life
Banksy, Asian-Style

Street artist Ernest Zacharevic (www.zachas.com) has been dubbed the Malaysian Banksy. Born in Lithuania and based in Penang, the 20-something artist has garnered a global following for his fantastically playful, interactive street art. Zacharevic's murals often incorporate real-life props, whether old bicycles, chairs, even the moss growing out of cracks. In one small work opposite the Malabar Muslim Jama-ath Mosque, two exhilarated kids freewheel it on a pair of 3D supermarket trolleys. To the right, a young boy somersaults out of a box, while further south on the corner of Victoria St and Jln Pisang, a giant girl caresses a lion cub.

85 Sultan Gate; adult/child under 6yr $4/free; ⊙10am-6pm Tue-Sun; Ⓜ Bugis)

KSB Ayurvedic Centre   MASSAGE

8 🎯 Map p96, B5

If Little India's hyperactive energy leaves you frazzled, revive the Indian way with an Ayurvedic (traditional Indian medicine) massage at this modest, friendly place. Treatments include Udwarthana (using a paste of herbs and grains to cleanse the skin and improve circulation) and the highly popular Abhyangam (synchronised massage using medicated oils). Yoga classes are also on offer. (☎6635 2339; www.ayurvedaksb.sg; 11 Upper Dickson Rd; 30min massage from S$35; ⊙9am-9pm Mon-Sat, to 3pm Sun; Ⓜ Little India)

Hajjah Fatimah Mosque   MOSQUE

9 🎯 Map p96, E7

Singapore's 'Leaning Tower of Pisa' is the minaret at this curious mosque, sloping about six degrees off centre due to the sandy soil on which the structure stands. The mosque itself is intriguing for its idiosyncratic architecture, which blends Middle Eastern and British styles. Among its features is a stained-glass dome roof. Constructed in 1846, the building is named after Melaka-born Singaporean philanthropist Hajjah Fatimah, whose home once stood on the site. (☎6297 2774; 4001 Beach Rd; ⊙9am-9pm; Ⓜ Nicoll Hwy, Lavender)

Malabar Muslim Jama-ath Mosque

MOSQUE

10 🔘 Map p96, E5

Architecture goes easy-wipe at the golden-domed Malabar Muslim Jama-ath Mosque, a curious creation clad entirely in striking blue geometric tiles. This is the only mosque on the island dedicated to Malabar Muslims from the South Indian state of Kerala, and though the building was commenced in 1956, it wasn't officially opened until 1963 due to cash-flow problems. The better-late-than-never motif continued with the tiling, which was only completed in 1995. (📞6294 3862; www.malabar.org.sg; 471 Victoria St; admission free; ⏰2.30-4pm & 5-6.30pm; Ⓜ Lavender)

Kuan Im Thong Hood Cho Temple

BUDDHIST TEMPLE

11 🔘 Map p96, B7

Awash with the frenetic click of *chien tung* (Chinese fortune sticks), this is one of Singapore's busiest (and according to devotees, luckiest) temples. It's dedicated to the goddess of mercy, Kuan Yin (Guan Yin), a much-loved bestower of good fortune. Flower-sellers and fortune tellers swarm around the entrance, while, further up the street, believers rub the belly of a large bronze Buddha Maitreya for extra luck. (178 Waterloo St; admission free; ⏰6am-6.30pm; Ⓜ Bugis)

Ⓠ Local Life
Petain Road Terraces

Between Jln Besar and Sturdee Rd is an extraordinary row of lavishly decorated double-storey **terraces** (Map p96, D2; Petain Rd; Ⓜ Farrer Park) dating back to the 1920s. They're a gasp-inducing explosion of colour, from the floral-motif ceramic wall tiles to the pillar bas-reliefs adorned with flowers, birds and trees. The hyper-ornate decoration is typical of what's known as Late Shophouse Style. The terraces are located an easy 500m walk east of Farrer Park MRT station.

St Gregory Javana Spa

SPA

12 🔘 Map p96, E8

The St Gregory group is a major player in the relaxation stakes, with four facilities in Singapore. This recently refurbished branch is at the Parkroyal hotel, its forest-inspired design a dreamy backdrop for treatments ranging from Swedish massage, wraps and milk baths to traditional Chinese therapies and oil-based Ayurvedic massage. (📞6505 5755; www.stgregoryspa. com; level 4, Parkroyal, 7500 Beach Rd; treatments S$45-300; ⏰10am-10pm Mon-Fri, 9am-9pm Sat & Sun; Ⓜ Bugis, Nicoll Hwy)

Hounds of the Baskervilles

GROOMING

13 🔘 Map p96, D7

Inked hipsters, antique cabinets bursting with clippers, and a hissing

CALVIN CHAN WAI MENG/GETTY IMAGES ©

Shop houses line the road to Sultan Mosque (p99)

espresso machine: no place screams new-school Singapore like this old-school-inspired barber–tattoo parlour. Get clippered or snipped (walk-ins only), or pimp your skin with a striking new design. The top-dog artist here is Rosman, a Javanese dude famed for his batik designs. (☎6299 1197; www.facebook.com/HoundsOfTheBaskervilles; 24A Bali Lane; buzz cut/full cut/shave S$15/40/35; ☺2.30-8pm Mon-Fri, to 7pm Sat; Ⓜ Bugis)

Nrityalaya Aesthetics Society

COURSE

14 ◎ Map p96, B8

Runs classes and workshops in traditional Indian arts such as classical dance, music, yoga and meditation. Also holds occasional performances.

The website isn't always kept up to date so call or pop in to the Stamford Arts Centre to see what's on when you're here. (☎6336 6537; www.nas.org.sg; Stamford Arts Centre, 155 Waterloo St; ☺10.30am-6.30pm Mon-Fri, 9am-7pm Sat & Sun; Ⓜ Bugis)

Eating

Kilo

FUSION $$$

15 ✕ Map p96, E5

Despite Singapore's cut-throat restaurant scene, gastro geeks remain loyal to this ode to fusion cooking. Expect the unexpected, from beef-tongue tacos with apple-miso slaw to goat-cheese and ricotta gnocchi with *maitake* mushrooms, brown-miso butter and *shiso* (a mint-like Asian herb). Slightly tricky to find, the restaurant occupies the 2nd floor of a lone industrial building on the Kallang River; take a taxi. (☑ after 4pm 6467 3987; www.kilokitchen.com; 66 Kampong Bugis; sharing plates S$15-28, mains S$26-48; ⏱ 6-10.15pm Mon-Sat; Ⓜ Lavender)

Lagnaa Barefoot Dining INDIAN $$

16 ⊗ Map p96, B5

You can choose your level of spice at friendly Lagnaa: level three denotes standard spiciness, level four significant spiciness, and anything above admirable bravery. Whatever you opt for, you're in for finger-licking-good homestyle cooking from both ends of Mother India, devoured at Western seating downstairs or on floor cushions upstairs. If you're indecisive, order chef Kaesavan's famous Threadfin fish curry. (☑ 6296 1215; www.lagnaa.com; 6 Upper Dickson Rd; dishes S$10-22; ⏱ 11.30am-10pm; 📶; Ⓜ Little India)

Cicheti ITALIAN $$

17 ⊗ Map p96, E7

Cool-kid Cicheti is a slick, friendly, buzzing scene of young-gun pizzaioli, trendy diners and seductive, contemporary Italian dishes made with hand-picked market produce. Tuck into beautifully charred woodfired pizzas, made-from-scratch pasta, and evening standouts like *polpette di carne grana* (slow-cooked meatballs topped with shaved Grana Padana). Book early in the week if heading in on a Friday or Saturday night. (☑ 6292 5012; www.cicheti.com; 52 Kandahar St; pizzas S$17-25, mains S$24-38; ⏱ noon-2.30pm & 6.30-10.30pm Mon-Fri, 6-10.30pm Sat; Ⓜ Bugis)

Zam Zam MALAYSIAN $

18 ⊗ Map p96, D7

These guys have been here since 1908, so they know what they're doing. Tenure hasn't bred complacency, though – the touts still try to herd customers in off the street, while frenetic chefs inside whip up delicious *murtabak,* the restaurant's speciality savoury pancakes, filled with succulent mutton, chicken, beef, venison or even sardines. (☑ 6298 6320; 699 North Bridge Rd; murtabak from S$5, dishes S$4-20; ⏱ 7am-11pm; Ⓜ Bugis)

Tekka Centre HAWKER $

19 ⊗ Map p96, A5

There's no shortage of subcontinental spice at this bustling hawker centre, wrapped around the sloshed guts and hacked bones of the wet market. Queue up for real-deal biryani, *dosa* (thin, lentil-flour pancake), *roti prata* (dough-flour pancake) and *teh tarik* (pulled tea). Well worth seeking out is **Ah-Rahman Royal Prata** (01-248, Tekka Centre, cnr Serangoon & Buffalo Rds; murtabak from S$5; ⏱ 7.30am-10.30pm Tue-Sun; Ⓜ Little India), which flips some of Singapore's finest *murtabak*. (cnr

Serangoon & Buffalo Rds; dishes S$3-10; ⏱7am-11pm; ✍; Ⓜ Little India)

Azmi Restaurant INDIAN $

20 🍴 Map p96, B4

This no-frills corner eatery is arguably the best place in Little India to sample freshly baked chapati. Choose from a string of curries, displayed buffet style, then decide how many chapatis you'll need to mop up your choice. Seating is of the plastic-stool variety, so don't bother wearing your Sunday best. Purchase drinks from the separate Chinese-run stall in the corner. (Norris Rd Chapati; 1 Norris Rd, cnr Serangoon Rd; dishes S$1.30-5.50, chapati S$0.90; ⏱7.30am-10.30pm; Ⓜ Little India)

Bismillah Biryani INDIAN $

21 🍴 Map p96, B6

This place is often touted as having the best biryani in Singapore, and the owners have taken it one step further by declaring that it's 'probably the best biryani anywhere!' Mutton biryani is the speciality – and it is special – but even that's surpassed by the melt-in-the-mouth mutton kebab. Get here early: the best dishes are often long gone before closing. (📞9382 7937; www.facebook.com/Bismillah-Biryani-Singapore-134575666639087/; 50 Dunlop St; kebabs from S$4, biryani from S$6; ⏱11.30am-3pm & 5.30-9pm Wed-Mon; Ⓜ Little India, Rochor)

Komala Vilas SOUTH INDIAN $

22 🍴 Map p96, B5

This prime-position branch of the Komala Vilas chain is extremely popular due to the wallet-friendly, authentic dishes and generous portions. Food can be spicy, so either ask the waiter to turn down the heat or order a mango lassi to calm the burn. (📞9826 6742; www.komalavilas.com.sg; 76-87 Serangoon Rd; dishes S$5-10; ⏱7am-10.30pm; ✍; Ⓜ Little India)

Warong Nasi Pariaman MALAYSIAN, INDONESIAN $

23 🍴 Map p96, E6

This no-frills corner *nasi padang* (rice with curries) stall is the stuff of legend. Top choices include the *belado* (fried mackerel in a slow-cooked chilli, onion and vinegar sauce), delicate *rendang* beef and *ayam bakar* (grilled chicken with coconut sauce). Get here by 11am to avoid the hordes. And be warned: most of it sells out by 1pm (10am Saturday). (📞6292 2374; www.pariaman.com.sg; 742 North Bridge Rd; dishes from S$4.50; ⏱8am-4pm; Ⓜ Bugis)

Cocotte FRENCH $$$

24 🍴 Map p96, C5

Never mind the Little India address, hip Cocotte is red, white and blue, down to its succulent French *jus*. Plan your next Gallic adventure over a platter of *charcuterie* (cold cooked meats), tender beef-short-rib *bourguignon* or the signature *poulet rôti* (a whole

People eating at Tekka Centre (p103)

chicken roasted to perfection and served with seasonal vegetables and rich pan juices). (📞6298 1188; www.restaurantcocotte.com; Wanderlust Hotel, 2 Dickson Rd; mains S$34-60; 🕑noon-2pm & 6.30-10pm Mon-Thu, noon-2.30pm & 6.30-10.30pm Fri-Sun; 🛜; Ⓜ Rochor)

Piedra Negra   MEXICAN $$

25 🍴 Map p96, E8

Sexy Latin beats, bombastic murals and tables right on free-spirited Haji Lane: this electric Mexican joint is a brilliant spot for cheapish cocktails and a little evening people-watching. Frozen or shaken, the margaritas pack a punch, and the joint's burritos, quesadillas, tacos and other Tex-Mex staples are filling and delish. (📞6291 1297; www.facebook.com/Piedra.Negra. Haji.Lane; cnr Beach Rd & Haji Lane; mains S$11.90-21.90; 🕑noon-12.30am Mon-Thu, noon-2am Fri & Sat; 🛜; Ⓜ Bugis)

Nan Hwa Chong Fish-Head Steamboat Corner   CHINESE $$

26 🍴 Map p96, E6

If you only try fish-head steamboat once, do it at this noisy, open-fronted veteran. Cooked on charcoal, the large pot of fish heads is brought to you in a steaming broth spiked with *tee po* (dried flat sole fish). One pot is enough for three or four people, and can stretch to more with rice and side dishes. (📞6297 9319; www.nanhwachong.com; 812-816 North Bridge Rd; fish steamboats from S$20; 🕑4pm-1am; Ⓜ Lavender)

Moghul Sweets

SWEETS $

If you're after a subcontinental sugar rush, tiny Moghul in the Little India Arcade (see 2 ⊙ Map p96, A5) is the place to get it. Bite into luscious *gulab jamun* (syrup-soaked fried dough balls), harder-to-find *rasmalai* (paneer cheese soaked in cardamom-infused clotted cream) and *barfi* (condensed milk and sugar slice) in flavours including pistachio, chocolate...and carrot. (⌚6392 5797; 01-16, Little India Arcade, 48 Serangoon Rd; sweets from S$1; ⊙9.30am-9.30pm; Ⓜ Little India)

Ananda Bhavan

INDIAN $

This super-cheap chain restaurant opposite the Tekka Centre (see 19 ⊙ Map p96, A5) is a top spot to sample South Indian breakfast staples like *idly* (fermented-rice cakes) and *dosa* (spelt 'thosai' on the menu). It also does great-value thali. There are other branches around Little India, all just as no-frills as this one, and all with the same commitment to dishing up tasty, healthy vegetarian food. (⌚6295 9895; www.anandabhavan.com; 58 Serangoon Rd; dosa S$2.60-5.20, set meals S$6-10; ⊙7.30am-10pm Mon-Thu, to 10.30pm Fri-Sun; ⌚; Ⓜ Little India)

Ya Kun Kaya Toast

CAFE $

27 ✕ Map p96, C8

In the basement food hall of Bugis Junction mall, this respected local chain is a solid spot for a traditional local breakfast of *kopi* (coffee) and *kaya* (coconut jam) toast. Don't forget

to add a splash of soy sauce and black pepper to the runny eggs before dunking your toast! Don't be put off by the queues – they usually move fast. (⌚6238 8904; www.yakun.com; B1-11, Bugis Junction, 230 Victoria St; kaya-toast set S$4.80; ⊙7.30am-10pm; Ⓜ Bugis)

Symmetry

CAFE $$

28 ✕ Map p96, E6

With rusty beams, random lamps and indie tunes, Symmetry feels like a garage made for band jams, but it's all about the grub, coffee and suds. Book for the weekend brunch, its wickedly good offerings including charred miso- and ginger-marinated mackerel, pork collar–stuffed croissants, and the satisfying Eggs Sur Le Plat (with pork sausage, smoked paprika, cherry-tomato coulis and creamed spinach). (⌚6291 9901; www.symmetry.com.sg; 9 Jln Kubor; brunch S$16-29; ⊙10.30am-9pm Mon, to 11pm Tue-Thu, to midnight Fri, 9am-midnight Sat, to 7pm Sun; 🛜; Ⓜ Bugis)

QS269 Food House

HAWKER $

29 ✕ Map p96, B8

This is not so much a 'food house' as a loud, crowded undercover laneway lined with cult-status stalls. Work up a sweat with a bowl of award-winning coconut-curry noodle soup from **Ah Heng** (www.facebook.com/AhHengChickenCurryNoodles; dishes from S$4; ⊙8am-4.30pm Sat-Thu) or join the queue at **New Rong Liang Ge** (Stall 01-235, dishes from S$2.50; ⊙9am-8pm), with succulent roast-duck dishes that draw foodies from across the city. The laneway's down the side of the building. (Block 269B, Queen St; ⏱individual stalls vary; M Bugis)

Drinking

Maison Ikkoku COCKTAIL BAR

30 🚇 Map p96, E7

Pimped with suspended dressers, Maison Ikkoku's cafe flies the flag for third-wave coffee, with options including Chemex, siphon, cold drip, V60, AeroPress and seasonal-blend espresso. The real magic happens in the upstairs cocktail bar, where a request for something sour might land you a tart, hot combo of spicy gin, grape, lemon and Japanese-chilli threads. Not cheap but well worth it. (☎6294 0078; www.maison-ikkoku.net; 20 Kandahar St; ⏱cafe 9am-9pm Mon-Thu, to 10pm Fri & Sat, to 7pm Sun, bar 6pm-1am Sun-Thu, to 2am Fri & Sat; 🛜; M Bugis)

Beast BAR

31 🚇 Map p96, E6

If you're after some hard liquor and only bourbon will do, pull up a stool at a rusty drum and start working your way through the Beast's grandiose selection, including home-brewed Southern Comfort. The kitchen churns out lip-smacking American Deep South–style food; the fried chicken and waffles is a standout. (☎6295 0017; www.thebeast.sg; 17 Jln Klapa; ⏱5pm-

midnight Mon-Wed & Sat, to 1am Thu & Fri, 10am-5pm Sun; M Bugis)

Artistry CAFE

32 🚇 Map p96, D7

Killer coffee, rotating art exhibitions and monthly after-hours events, including singer-songwriter nights; Artistry is

---

Q Local Life

Jalan Besar

Once better known for its hardware stores and boxing matches, Jalan Besar is metamorphosing into an area where heritage architecture meets new-school Singapore cool. It's a compact district, centred on Jalan Besar and Tyrwhitt Rd. It's on the latter that you'll find cult-status cafe-roaster **Chye Seng Huat Hardware** (☎6396 0609; www.cshhcoffee.com; 150 Tyrwhitt Rd; ⏱9am-7pm Tue-Fri, to 10pm Sat & Sun; M Farrer Park, Lavender).

Right above it sits Tyrwhitt General Company, a shop-workshop peddling handmade jewellery, art and knickknacks. If it's late afternoon, cool down at nearby beer joint **Druggists** (☎6341 5967; www.facebook.com/DruggistsSG; 119 Tyrwhitt Rd; ⏱4pm-midnight Tue-Fri, noon-midnight Sat & Sun; M Farrer Park, Lavender). Its 23 taps pour a rotating selection of craft brews from microbreweries around the world.

To reach Jalan Besar, alight at Lavendar MRT and walk northwest up Horne Rd to Tyrwhitt Rd.

Graffiti decorates the walls of Piedra Negra (p105) on Haji Lane

DOUBLEPHOTO STUDIO/SHUTTERSTOCK ©

a hipster version of the cultural salon. Swig interesting artisanal beers and ciders or tuck into fresh, delicious grub (served till 5pm) like guilt-inducing BRB (blueberry, ricotta and bacon) pancakes or the cross-cultural chilli-crab burger. (☑6298 2420; www.artistryspace. com; 17 Jln Pinang; ☉9am-11pm Tue-Sat, to 4pm Sun; ☜; ⓜBugis)

Bar Stories   COCKTAIL BAR

33 🍸 Map p96, D7

Call ahead if heading in later in the week – this upstairs cocktail den is as small as it's hugely popular. If you're lucky you'll be sitting at the bar, where gung-ho barkeeps keep it freestyle, turning whatever spirit or flavour turns you on into a smashing libation.

Creative, whimsical and often brilliant. (☑6298 0838; 55/57A Haji Lane; ☉4pm-1am Sun-Thu, to 2am Fri & Sat; ⓜBugis)

Prince of Wales   PUB

34 🍸 Map p96, B5

The closest thing to a pub in Little India, this grungy Aussie hang-out is an affable, popular spot, with a small beer garden, a pool table and sports screens. Weekly staples include Wednesday quiz night (from 8pm) and free-flow house pours on Thursday night (gents/ladies S$28/24). Doubles as a **hostel** (dm/d S$20/60; ✻@☜). (☑6299 0130; www.pow.com.sg; 101 Dunlop St; ☉9am-1am Sun-Thu, to 2am Fri & Sat; ⓜLittle India, Rochor).

Entertainment

Going Om
LIVE MUSIC

35 ⭐ Map p96, D7

Right on Haji Lane, Going Om is a raffish, free-spirited cafe with nightly live music. It's an atmospheric spot, with candlelit tables, smooth acoustic sets (mostly well-executed covers) and no shortage of carefree punters dancing in the laneway. The boho spirit extends to the beverage list, which includes 'chakra' drinks of seven colours (one for each chakra, dude). (☑6396 3592; www.going-om.com.sg; 63 Haji Lane; ⏱5.30pm-1am Tue-Thu, 5.30pm-3am Fri, 3.30pm-3am Sat, 3.30pm-1am Sun; Ⓜ Bugis)

BluJaz Café
LIVE MUSIC

36 ⭐ Map p96, D7

Bohemian pub BluJaz is one of the best options in town for live music, with regular jazz jams, and other acts playing anything from blues to rockabilly. Check the website for the list of events, which includes DJ-spun funk, R&B and retro nights, as well as 'Talk Cock' open-mic comedy nights on Wednesday and Thursday. Cover charge for some shows. (☑9199 0610; www.blujazcafe.net; 11 Bali Lane; ⏱noon-1am Mon-Thu, to 2am Fri, 3pm-2am Sat; 📶; Ⓜ Bugis)

SingJazz Club
JAZZ

37 ⭐ Map p96, E6

Good sax, crooners and the occasional dose of soul, funk, Latin and house is what you get at this intimate jazz bar, with both local and visiting acts taking to its red-curtained stage. Leave the shorts and flip-flops at your hotel. Check the club's Facebook page for upcoming gigs. (☑8481 3034; www.facebook.com/singjazzclub; Sultan Hotel, 101 Jln Sultan; ⏱9pm-1am Wed-Sun; Ⓜ Bugis)

Hood
LIVE MUSIC

38 ⭐ Map p96, C8

Inside the Bugis+ mall, Hood's street-art interior sets a youthful scene for nightly music jams with acts such as Rush Hour and Smells Like Last Friday. If it's undiscovered talent you're after, the weekly 'Saturday Original Sessions' is a showcase for budding musos itching to share their singer-songwriter skills. (☑6221 8846;

◯ Local Life
Bollywood at the Rex

Where can you catch the Bollywood blockbusters advertised all over Little India? Why at the **Rex Cinemas** (Map p97, A6; http://tickets.rexcinema.com.sg; 2 Mackenzie Rd; tickets $13; ⓂLittle India), of course. This historic theatre, on the very edge of the neighbourhood, screens films from around the subcontinent, most subtitled in English.

www.hoodbarandcafe.com; 05-07, Bugis+, 201 Victoria St; ☻5pm-1am Mon-Wed, to 3am Thu & Fri, noon-3am Sat, to 1am Sun; ⓂBugis)

Singapore Dance Theatre　DANCE

`39` ⭐ Map p96, C8

This is the HQ of Singapore's premier dance company, which keeps fans swooning with its repertoire of classic ballets and contemporary works, many of which are performed at Esplanade – Theatres on the Bay (p43). The true highlight is the group's Ballet under the Stars season at Fort Canning Park (p32), which usually runs in June or July. See the website for program details. (☏6338 0611; www.singaporedancetheatre.com; Level 7, Bugis+, 201 Victoria St; ⓂBugis)

Wild Rice　THEATRE

`40` ⭐ Map p96, A4

Singapore's sexiest theatre group is based in Kerbau Rd but performs shows elsewhere in the city (as well as abroad). A mix of homegrown and foreign work, productions range from farce to serious politics, fearlessly wading into issues not commonly on the agenda in Singapore. (☏6292 2695; www.wildrice.com.sg; 65 Kerbau Rd; ⓂLittle India)

Shopping

Sifr Aromatics　PERFUME

`41` 🔒 Map p96, E8

This Zen-like perfume laboratory belongs to third-generation perfumer Johari Kazura, whose exquisite creations include the heady East (50mL S$185), a blend of oud, rose absolute, amber and neroli. The focus is on custom-made fragrances (consider calling ahead to arrange an appointment), with other heavenly offerings including affordable, high-quality body balms, scented candles and vintage perfume bottles. (☏6392 1966; www.sifr.sg; 42 Arab St; ☻11am-8pm Mon-Sat, to 5pm Sun; ⓂBugis, Nicoll Hwy)

Supermama　GIFTS & SOUVENIRS

`42` 🔒 Map p96, E8

Tucked around the corner from Arab St, this gallery-esque store is a treasure trove of contemporary giftware. Crunch around on the quirky gravel floor while you pore over the Singapore-inspired wares, most created by local designers. The blue-and-white fine-porcelain dishes, made in Japan, are the headliners.

Additional branches are located at the Singapore Art Museum (p32) and Esplanade Mall. (☏6291 1946; www.supermama.sg; 265 Beach Rd; ☻11am-8pm; ⓂBugis)

GRACETHANG2/SHUTTERSTOCK ©

Haji Lane fashion shops (p113)

Tuckshop & Sundry Supplies
FASHION & ACCESSORIES

43 Map p96, D7

A vintage-inspired ode to American working-class culture, this little menswear store offers a clued-in selection of rugged threads and accessories, including designer eyewear, grooming products and made-in-house leather goods. Stock up on plaid shirts, sweat tops and harder-to-find denim from brands like Japan's Iron Heart and China's Red Cloud. (☎6396 4568; www.tuckshop-sundrysupplies.com; 25 Bali Lane; ⏰11am-9pm Mon-Sat, noon-6pm Sun; MBugis)

Little Shophouse
ARTS & CRAFTS

44 Map p96, E7

Traditional Peranakan beadwork is a dying art, but it's kept very much alive in this shop and workshop. The shop's colourful slippers are designed by craftsman Robert Sng and are hand-beaded by himself and his sister, Irene. While they're not cheap (circa S$1000), each pair takes a painstaking 100 hours to complete. You'll also find Peranakan-style tea sets, crockery, vases, handbags and jewellery. (☎6295 2328; 43 Bussorah St; ⏰10am-6pm; MBugis)

Understand

The Sinagporean Table

Food is one of Singapore's greatest drawcards, the nation's melting pot of cultures creating one of the world's most diverse, drool-inducing culinary landscapes.

Chinese

Thank the Hainanese for Hainanese chicken rice (steamed fowl and rice cooked in chicken stock, served with a clear soup and a chilli-ginger dip), and the Hokkiens for *hokkien mee* (yellow Hokkien noodles with prawns) and *char kway teow* (stir-fried noodles with cockles, Chinese sausage and dark sauces). Teochew cuisine is famed for its rice porridge, while Cantonese classics include *won ton* soup.

Malaysian & Indonesian

Feast on Katong laksa (spicy coconut curry broth with noodles, prawns, cockles, fish cake, bean sprouts and laksa leaf), *ikan assam* (fried fish in a sour tamarind curry) and *nasi lemak* (coconut rice with fried fish and peanuts). Equally mouth-watering is *nasi padang,* which sees steamed rice paired with a choice of meat and vegetable dishes such as *sambal tofu-tempeh* (spicy tofu and fermented beans).

Peranakan

Peranakan (Nonya) food is a cross-cultural fusion of Chinese and Malay influences. Dishes are tangy, spicy and commonly flavoured with chillies, shallots, *belacan* (Malay fermented prawn paste), preserved soya beans, peanuts, coconut milk and galangal (a ginger-like root). Classics include *otak-otak,* a sausage-like blend of fish, coconut milk, chilli paste, galangal and herbs grilled in a banana leaf.

Indian

South India's hot flavours dominate. Tuck into thali, a combination of rice, curries, *rasam* (hot, sour soup) and dessert served on a banana leaf. Leave room for *roti prata* (fried flat bread served with curry sauce), *masala dosa* (thin pancake filled with spiced potatoes and chutney), and halal (Muslim) *murtabak* (lightly grilled dough stuffed with onion and seasoned meat, usually mutton).

Sim Lim Square   ELECTRONICS, MALL

45 🔒 Map p96, B6

A byword for all that is cut-price and geeky, Sim Lim is jammed with stalls selling laptops, cameras, soundcards and games consoles. If you know what you're doing there are deals to be had, but the untutored are likely to be out of their depth. Bargain hard (yet politely) and always check that the warranty is valid in your home country. (☏6338 3859; www.simlimsquare. com.sg; 1 Rochor Canal Rd; ⏱10.30am-9pm; Ⓜ Rochor)

Bugis Street Market   MARKET

46 🔒 Map p96, C8

What was once Singapore's most infamous sleaze pit – packed with foreign servicemen on R&R, gambling dens and 'sisters' (transvestites) – is now its most famous undercover street market, crammed with cheap clothes, shoes, accessories and manicurists and especially popular with teens and 20-somethings. In a nod to its past, there's even a sex shop. (☏6338 9513; www.bugisstreet.com.sg; 3 Bugis St; ⏱11am-10pm; Ⓜ Bugis)

🔍 Local Life

Haji Lane

Narrow, pastel Haji Lane (Map p97, E8) harbours a handful of quirky boutiques. Girly threads get a little indie edge at **Soon Lee** (☏6297 0198; www.facebook.com/soonlee.singapore; 73 Haji Lane; ⏱noon-9pm; Ⓜ Bugis), while concept store **Mondays Off** (www.mondays-off.com; 76 Haji Lane; ⏱noon-8pm Tue-Fri, from 10am Sat & Sun; Ⓜ Bugis) stocks anything from contemporary local ceramics and funky cushions to art mags and geometric racks to store them on.

Mustafa Centre   DEPARTMENT STORE

47 🔒 Map p96, C3

Little India's bustling Mustafa Centre is a magnet for budget shoppers, most of them from the subcontinent. It's a sprawling place, selling everything from electronics and garish gold jewellery to shoes, bags, luggage and beauty products. There's also a large supermarket with a great range of Indian foodstuffs. If you can't handle crowds, avoid the place on Sunday. (www.mustafa.com.sg; 145 Syed Alwi Rd; ⏱24hr; Ⓜ Farrer Park)

Explore

Sentosa Island

Epitomised by its star attraction, Universal Studios, Sentosa is essentially one giant Pleasure Island. The choices are head-spinning, from duelling roller coasters and indoor skydiving to stunt shows and luge racing. Add to this a historic fort, state-of-the-art aquarium and Ibiza-inspired beachside bars and restaurants, and it's clear why locals head here to live a little.

The Sights in a Day

☀ Only the truly insane would attempt to experience all of Sentosa's attractions in one day, so choose a few and enjoy them thoroughly. You could easily spend the entire day lapping up the rides, shows, food and shops at blockbuster Hollywood theme park **Universal Studios** (p116).

☀ Feast on Malay hawker favourites at **Malaysian Food Street** (p122), then spend the afternoon at Universal Studios. Alternatively, explore the deep at **SEA Aquarium** (p119), brush up on your local history at **Fort Siloso** (p120) or let the little ones loose at **KidZania** (p121). Adrenalin junkie options include indoor skydiving at **iFly** (p119) and luge racing at **Skyline Luge Sentosa** (p121), while those who prefer their thrills dripping wet should head to **Wave House** (p120).

☾ Slide into evening with sunset mojitos or beers at **Coastes** (p123) or **Tanjong Beach Club** (p122), then dine marina-side at **Mykonos on the Bay** (p122). For shameless romance and a fine-dining menu, however, reserve a table at hilltop **Il Lido at the Cliff** (p121).

👁 Top Sights
Universal Studios (p116)

❤ Best of Singapore
Food & Drink
Il Lido at the Cliff (p121)

Malaysian Food Street (p122)

Knolls (p122)

Tanjong Beach Club (p122)

Thrills & Spills
Universal Studios (p116)

iFly (p119)

Wave House (p120)

Getting There

🚡 **Cable car** Ride the cable car from Mt Faber or the HarbourFront Centre. (On Sentosa, a separate cable-car line stops at Imbiah Lookout, Merlion and Siloso Point.)

🚉 **Monorail** The Sentosa Express (7am to midnight) connects VivoCity to three stations on Sentosa: Waterfront, Imbiah and Beach.

🚶 **Walk** Simply walk across the Sentosa Boardwalk from VivoCity.

Top Sights
Universal Studios

Hankering for a little unadulterated fun? Then Universal Studios is looking at you, kid. The top-draw attraction at Resorts World, its booty of rides, roller coasters, shows, shops and restaurants are neatly packaged into fantasy-world themes based on your favourite Hollywood films. Attractions span the toddler-friendly to the seriously gut-wrenching, spread across a storybook landscape of castles, temples, jungles, retro Americana and sci-fi fantasy.

👁 Map p118, D2

📞 6577 8888

www.rwsentosa.com

Resorts World, 8 Sentosa Gateway

adult/child S$74/54

🕐 10am-6pm

Ⓜ HarbourFront, then monorail to Waterfront

Don't Miss

Battlestar Galactica

If you're a hard-core thrill seeker, strap yourself into Battlestar Galactica, which consists of the world's tallest duelling roller coasters. Choose between the sit-down HUMAN roller coaster and the CYLON, an inverted roller coaster with multiple loops and flips. If you can pull your attention away from the (yours and others') screaming, be sure to enjoy the bird's-eye view.

Transformers: The Ride

This exhilarating, next-generation motion thrill ride deploys high-definition 3D animation to transport you to a dark, urban other-world where you'll be battling giant robots, engaging in high-speed chases, and even plunging off the edge of a soaring skyscraper. It's an incredibly realistic, adrenaline-pumping experience.

Revenge of the Mummy

The main attraction of the park's Ancient Egypt section, Revenge of the Mummy will have you twisting, dipping and hopping in darkness in your search for the Book of the Living. Contrary to Hollywood convention, your journey will end with a surprising, fiery twist.

Puss in Boots' Giant Journey

Perfect for little kids, this suspended roller coaster takes you on a fairly tame ride with Puss in Boots and his girlfriend, Kitty Softpaws, in search of Mother Goose's precious golden egg. The attention to detail is wonderful; sit in the last row for more of a thrill.

☑ Top Tips

▶ If lining up isn't your thing, consider investing in an express pass (S$50), which lets you jump in the fast lane for each participating ride once.

▶ Friday to Sunday is busiest, Wednesday morning is generally quietest. Avoid public holidays.

▶ Consider wearing flip-flops, especially if hitting water-themed rides.

✕ Take a Break

For those travelling with a tribe, head to **Loui's NY Pizza Parlor** (20-inch pizza S$49).

Just outside the Universal Studios entrance is Malaysian Food Street (p122). Make sure to get a wristband if you want to re-enter the theme park.

Pulau Brani

Brani Terminal Ave

Selat Sengkir

Causeway Bridge

Sentosa Gateway

1 SEA Aquarium

Gateway Ave

Resorts World

Universal Studios

Serapong Golf Course

Allanbrooke Rd

10

Tanjong Golf Course

Bukit Manis Rd

9

11 Tanjong Beach

The Knolls

Artillery Ave

KidZania

7

Imbiah

Waterfront

Merlion Plaza

Beach View

Palawan Beach

Keppel Harbour

Sentosa Cable Car Station

Images of Singapore Live

Cable Car Rd

5

2 iFly

Beach

Skyline Luge Sentosa

13

8

12

Siloso Rd

Mt Imbiah

Imbiah Walk

Wave House

4

Siloso Beach

MegaZip

6

Sebarok Channel

3 Fort Siloso

500 m
0.25 miles

For reviews see

◆	Top Sights	p116
◎	Sights	p119
✖	Eating	p121
☗	Drinking	p122
☻	Entertainment	p123

VOLODYMYR GOINYK/GETTY IMAGES ©

Tropical fish at SEA Aquarium

Sights

SEA Aquarium AQUARIUM

1 ◉ Map p118, D1

You'll be gawking at over 800 species of aquatic creature at Singapore's impressive, sprawling aquarium. The state-of-the-art complex recreates 49 aquatic habitats found between Southeast Asia, Australia and Africa. The Open Ocean habitat is especially spectacular, its 36m-long, 8.3m-high viewing panel one of the world's largest. The complex is also home to an interactive, family-friendly exhibition exploring the history of the maritime Silk Route. (☏6577 8888; www.rwsentosa.com; Resorts World, 8 Sentosa Gateway; adult/child under 13yr S\$32/22; ◷10am-7pm; Ⓜ HarbourFront, then monorail to Waterfront)

iFly ADVENTURE SPORTS

2 ◉ Map p118, C2

If you fancy free-falling from 3660m to 914m *without* leaping out of a plane, leap into this indoor-skydiving centre. The price includes an hour's instruction followed by two short but thrilling skydives in a vertical wind chamber. Tickets purchased two days in advance for off-peak times are significantly cheaper. See the website for details. (☏6571 0000; www.iflysingapore.com; 43 Siloso Beach Walk; 2 skydives S\$119; ◷9am-9.30pm Thu-Tue, from 11am Wed; Ⓜ HarbourFront, then monorail to Beach)

Top Tip

Tram & Buses

Shuttling the length of Sentosa's three beaches – Siloso, Palawan and Tanjong – the Sentosa 'beach tram' (electric bus) runs from 9am to 10.30pm Sunday to Friday, and from 9am to midnight Saturday. Three colour-coded bus routes link the main attractions. Buses 1 and 3 run from 8am to 10.30pm daily, and bus 2 runs from 9am to 10.30pm daily. All routes depart from the bus stop just east of Beach monorail station. The monorail, tram and buses are free.

Fort Siloso

MUSEUM

3 ⊙ Map p118, A1

Dating from the 1880s, when Sentosa was called Pulau Blakang Mati (Malay for 'the island behind which lies death'), this British coastal fort was famously useless during the Japanese invasion of 1942. Documentaries, artefacts, animatronics and recreated historical scenes take visitors through the fort's history, and the underground tunnels are fun to explore. Buy tickets to the Surrender Rooms to witness two pivotal moments in Singapore's history: the surrender of the British to the Japanese in 1942, and the reverse in 1945. (☑6736 8672; www.sentosa.com.sg; Siloso Point, Siloso Rd; free, Surrender Chambers adult/child under 13yr S$6/4.50; ⊘10am-6pm, last entry 5.30pm; Ⓜ HarbourFront, then monorail to Beach, then bus 1 or 2 to Siloso Point)

Wave House

SURFING

4 ⊙ Map p118, B2

Two specially designed wave pools allow surfer types to practise their gashes and cutbacks at ever-popular Wave House. The non-curling Double Flowrider is good for beginners, while the 3m FlowBarrel is more challenging. Wave House also includes beachside eating and drinking options. (☑6238 1196; www.wavehousesentosa.com; 36 Siloso Beach Walk; 30min FlowBarrel surf session S$30, 1hr Double Flowrider surf session from S$35; ⊘10.30am-10.30pm; Ⓜ HarbourFront, then monorail to Beach)

Images of Singapore Live

MUSEUM

5 ⊙ Map p118, C2

Using actors, immersive exhibitions and dramatic light-and-sound effects, Images of Singapore Live resuscitates the nation's history, from humble Malay fishing village to bustling colonial port and beyond. Young kids will especially love the Spirit of Singapore Boat Ride, a trippy, high-tech journey that feels just a little *Avatar*. Tickets purchased online are S$10 cheaper. (☑6715 4000; www.imagesofsingaporelive.com; 40 Imbiah Rd; adult/child under 13yr incl Madame Tussauds S$39/29; ⊘10am-6pm Mon-Fri, to 7.30pm Sat & Sun; Ⓜ HarbourFront, then monorail to Imbiah)

MegaZip ADVENTURE SPORTS

6 ◉ Map p118, B2

Part of the MegaAdventure playground, this 450m-long, 75m-tall zip-line runs from Imbiah Lookout to a tiny island off Siloso Beach. Alternatively, you can conquer the 15m drop in the Leap of Faith or head up instead of down on NorthFace, the 16m climbing wall. There's also a high-ropes adventure course, which will have you feeling like Tarzan, but with a harness. (www.megazip.com.sg; Imbiah Hill Rd; zip-line ride S$39.90; ☺11am-7pm; MHarbourFront, then monorail to Beach

KidZania AMUSEMENT PARK

7 ◉ Map p118, C2

Young ones get to be the grown-ups in this huge, indoor, kid-sized city. Comprising different 'workplaces', kids can try out their dream jobs, from airplane pilot to candy-design trainee – even crime-scene investigator. Parents can only watch, which means waiting around, but it's worth it to see your kid become a firefighter. Weekends are particularly busy. (☏1800 653 6888; www.kidzania.com.sg; 01-01/02 Palawan Kidz City, 31 Beach View; adult/child under 18yr/toddler 2-3yr S$58/35/25; ☺10am-5pm Sun-Thu, to 8pm Fri & Sat)

Skyline Luge Sentosa ADVENTURE SPORTS

8 ◉ Map p118, C2

Take the sky-ride chairlift from Siloso Beach to Imbiah Lookout, then hop

Surfer at Wave House

onto your luge (think go-cart meets toboggan) and race family and friends around hairpin bends and along bone-shaking straights carved through the forest (helmets are provided and mandatory). Young kids will love this. Those with heart conditions or bad backs won't. (☏6274 0472; www.skylineluge.com; 45 Siloso Beach Walk; luge & skyride combo from S$18; ☺10am-9.30pm; MHarbourFront, then monorail to Beach)

Eating

Il Lido at the Cliff INTERNATIONAL $$$

9 ✖ Map p118, E4

Perched high above Palawan Beach (although tree cover obscures some of the view), fine-dining Il Lido at the

Local Life
Brunch at Knolls

Free-flow-alcohol Sunday brunch is huge in Singapore, and posh, secluded **Knolls** (Map p118, D3; ☎6591 5046; www.capellahotels.com/singapore; Capella, 1 The Knolls; Sun brunch from S$128, children's meals from S$48; ⏱7am-11pm, Sun brunch 12.30-3pm; Ⓜ HarbourFront, then monorail to Beach, then bus 3 to Ranger Station) serves one of the best (S$148). Style up and join strutting peacocks, roaming band and a see-and-be-seen crowd for scrumptious buffet bites like freshly shucked oysters, blue-cheese and pumpkin liégeois, and foie-gras brûlée.

Cliff is set by the dreamy swimming-pool area of the luxury Sofitel hotel. Book two weeks ahead to secure a coveted table by the balcony's edge, an especially evocative spot to savour classic Italian dishes, paired with new- and old-world wines. (☎6708 8310; www.sofitel-singapore-sentosa.com; Sofitel Sentosa Resort & Spa, 2 Bukit Manis Rd; mains S$28-48; ⏱noon-2.30pm & 6-9.30pm; Ⓜ HarbourFront, then monorail to Beach, then bus 3)

Malaysian Food Street   HAWKER $

With its faux-Malaysian streetscape, this indoor hawker centre beside Universal Studios (see 1 Ⓜ Map p118, D1) feels a bit Disney. Thankfully, there's nothing fake about the food, cooked by some of Malaysia's best hawker vendors. (www.rwsentosa.com; Resorts World; dishes from S$5; ⏱11am-10pm Mon-Thu, 9am-11pm Fri & Sat, 9am-10pm Sun; Ⓜ HarbourFront, then monorail to Waterfront)

Mykonos on the Bay   GREEK $$

10 🍴 Map p118, E3

At Sentosa Cove, this slick, marina-flanking taverna serves up Hellenic flavours that could make your *papou* weep. Sit alfresco and tuck into perfectly charred, marinated octopus, aubergine spread and house-made *giaourtlou* (spicy lamb sausage). Book ahead later in the week. (☎6334 3818; www.mykonosonthebay.com; 01-10 Quayside Isle, 31 Ocean Way; tapas S$9-27, mains S$23-48; ⏱6-10.30pm Mon-Wed, noon-2.30pm & 6-10.30pm Thu & Fri, noon-10.30pm Sat & Sun; 🍴; Ⓜ HarbourFront, then monorail to Beach, then bus 3)

Drinking

Tanjong Beach Club   BAR

11 🍸 Map p118, E4

Generally cooler and scenier than the bars on Siloso Beach, Tanjong Beach Club is an evocative spot, with evening torches on the sand, a small, stylish pool for guests, and a sultry, lounge-and-funk soundtrack. The restaurant serves trendy beachside fare, and a kick-ass weekend-brunch menu. Sunday sees the decks come alive with DJs and dancing. (☎9750 5323; www.tanjongbeachclub.com; 120 Tanjong Beach Walk; ⏱11am-10pm Tue-Fri, 10am-11pm Sat & Sun; Ⓜ HarbourFront, then monorail to Beach, then tram to Tanjong Beach)

Siloso Beach

Coastes BAR

12 🚇 Map p118, B2

More family friendly than many of the other beach venues, Coastes has picnic tables on the palm-studded sand and sunloungers (S$20) by the water. There's a comprehensive menu of standard offerings, including burgers, pasta and salads. (📞6631 8938; www. coastes.com; 50 Siloso Beach Walk; ⏰9am-11pm Sun-Thu, to 1am Fri & Sat; Ⓜ Harbour-Front, then monorail to Beach)

Entertainment

Wings of Time THEATRE

13 ⭐ Map p118, C3

Set above the ocean, this ambitious show fuses Lloyd Webber–esque theatricality with an awe-inspiring sound, light and laser extravaganza. Prepare to gasp, swoon and (occasionally) cringe. (📞6736 8672; www. wingsoftime.com.sg; Siloso Beach; standard/ premium seats S$18/23; ⏰shows 7.40pm & 8.40pm; 🚈HarbourFront, then monorail to Beach)

Top Sights
Singapore Zoo

Getting There

Singapore Zoo is 22km northwest of the CBD.

Ⓜ **MRT** Catch the North-South (red) line to Ang Mo Kio, then bus 138 to the zoo.

Singapore Zoo is a verdant, tropical wonderland of spacious, naturalistic enclosures, freely roaming animals and interactive attractions. Breakfast with orang-utans, dodge flying foxes, mosey up to tree-hugging sloths, even snoop around a replica African village. Then there's the setting: 26 soothing hectares on a tranquil, bucolic peninsula jutting out onto the calm waters of the Upper Seletar Reservoir. A Singapore must-do.

Don't Miss

Jungle Breakfast with Wildlife

Orang-utans (pictured) are the zoo's celebrity residents and you can devour a breakfast buffet with them at **Jungle Breakfast with Wildlife** (Ah Meng Restaurant; ⏱9-10.30am). If you miss out, get your photo taken with them at the neighbouring Free Ranging Orang-utan Island (11am and 3.30pm). Best of all, you can use your own camera.

Fragile Forest

This giant bio-dome replicates the stratas of a rainforest. Cross paths with free-roaming butterflies and colourful lories, swooping Malayan flying foxes and unperturbed ring-tailed lemurs. The pathway leads up to the forest canopy and the dome's most chilled-out locals, the two-toed sloths.

Great Rift Valley of Ethiopia

Featuring cliffs, a waterfall and a stream fashioned to look like the Ethiopian hinterland, the evocative Great Rift Valley exhibit is home to Hamadryas baboons, Nubian ibexes, banded mongooses, black-backed jackals and rock hyraxes. You'll also find replica Ethiopian villages with dwelling huts and insight into the area's harsh living conditions.

Rainforest Kidzworld

Let your own little critters go wild at **Rainforest Kidzworld** (carousel/pony rides per person S$4/6), a play area with slides, swings, pulling boats and a carousel. Kids can also ride ponies (must be over 120cm tall), feed farmyard animals and squeal away in the wet-play area. Swimwear is available for purchase on-site.

☎6269 3411

www.zoo.com.sg

80 Mandai Lake Rd

adult/child under 13yr
S$33/22

⏱8.30am-6pm

Ⓜ Ang Mo Kio, then bus 138

☑ Top Tips

▶ Consider combining your trip with a visit to the neighbouring Night Safari.

▶ Wear comfortable shoes, a sun hat and sunglasses. Ponchos are available (S$5) in case of rain. If you have kids, bring swimwear for Rainforest Kidzworld.

▶ Feeding times are staggered. Check the website for details.

✗ Take a Break

There's no shortage of eateries on-site, serving everything from American fast food to local staples like laksa and *nasi lemak* (rice boiled in coconut milk with *ikan bilis* (anchovies fried whole), peanuts and a curry dish).

Top Sights
Night Safari

Getting There

Located beside the
Singapore Zoo, Night
Safari is 22km north-
west of the CBD.

M MRT Catch the
North-South (red) line
to Ang Mo Kio, then
bus 138 to the zoo.

Singapore's acclaimed Night Safari offers a different
type of nightlife. Home to over 120 species of animals, the park's barriers seem to melt away in the
darkness, giving you the feeling of being up close
with the likes of lions, leopards and alligators. The
atmosphere is heightened by strolling antelopes,
often passing within inches of the trams you're
travelling in.

Don't Miss

Electric Tram Tour

The Night Safari's open-sided vehicles come with a guide whose commentary is a good introduction to the park's animals and different habitats. The journey lasts for 45 minutes, though we highly recommend that you alight at the designated stops to explore more of the park on foot. If possible, opt for the second or third cars for the best views.

Walking Trails

The grounds offer four interlinked walking trails, each taking between 20 and 30 minutes to explore. Get centimetres away from wild spotted felines on the Leopard Trail, also home to the thrilling Giant Flying Squirrel aviary. Peer at splash-happy cats and the world's largest bat, the Malay flying fox, on the Fishing Cat Trail. The Wallaby Trail is home to a walk-through wallaby habitat, while the outstanding East Lodge Trail houses highly endangered babirusas and elegant Malay tigers.

Creatures of the Night

If you have kids in tow, **Creatures of the Night** (⊘7.30pm, 8.30pm, 9.30pm & 10.30pm) is an interactive 20-minute show with stars that include binturongs, civets and an owl. Seating is unassigned, so arrive a little early to secure a good vantage point. Shows may be cancelled in case of wet weather. Animal performances have been criticised by animal-welfare groups, who say that captivity is debilitating and stressful for animals, and that this is exacerbated by human interaction.

☏ 6269 3411

www.nightsafari.com.sg

80 Mandai Lake Rd

adult/child under 13yr
S$45/30

⊘ 7.15pm-midnight, restaurants & shops from 5.30pm

Ⓜ Ang Mo Kio, then bus 138

☑ Top Tips

▶ When returning, catch a bus at around 10.35pm as the last MRT train leaves Ang Mo Kio at 11.35pm. A taxi to the city centre is around S$23.

▶ Wear comfy shoes and bring insect repellent and an umbrella, just in case.

✗ Take a Break

Food and drink options abound outside the entrance. **Bongo Burgers** (mains S$12-16; ⊘5.30pm-midnight) serves tasty burgers using preservative-free meat.

Explore

Holland Village, Dempsey Hill & the Botanic Gardens

Chic, salubrious Holland Village may not be a must for visitors, but its boutiques, cafes and lunching ladies offer a revealing glimpse into expat life. Leafier still is historic Dempsey Hill, a converted barracks punctuated with antiques dealers, boutiques, cafes and relaxed bistros. Upstaging both neighbourhoods is the Botanic Gardens (pictured), an invigorating oasis of rare orchids and precious rainforest.

The Sights in a Day

☼ Beat the heat with an early morning saunter through the **Singapore Botanic Gardens** (p130), keeping cool in the ancient rainforest, circling Swan Lake and dropping in on Vanda Miss Joaquim, Singapore's national flower, at the National Orchid Centre. Appetite piqued, head across to **Long Beach Seafood** (p134) for their famous black pepper crab or join ladies who lunch at casual-chic **PS Cafe** (p135) for beautiful global fare.

☼ Spend the afternoon shop-hopping Dempsey Hill for antiques, art and accessories at stores like **Shang Antique** (p138) and **Em Gallery** (p139). If a little pampering is in order, book a facial or massage at heavenly **Spa Esprit** (p134), also in Dempsey. Alternatively, pop into fellow expat enclave Holland Village to gift shop at **Bynd Artisan** (p138) and sip a coffee, beer or vino at **Park** (p137).

☾ Come evening, opt for sundowners and Indonesian bites at heady, resort-like **Blue Bali** (p135). If the night is still young, head back to Dempsey for drinks and conversation at buzzing garden bar **Green Door** (p136) or local craft beer at laid-back **RedDot Brewhouse** (p137).

👁 Top Sights

Singapore Botanic Gardens (p130)

🖤 Best of Singapore

Food

Long Beach Seafood (p134)

PS Cafe (p135)

Blue Bali (p135)

Drinking

Green Door (p136)

RedDot Brewhouse (p137)

Shopping

Shang Antique (p138)

Bynd Artisan (p138)

Getting There

Ⓜ **MRT** The Botanic Gardens and Holland Village both have their own MRT stations.

🚌 **Bus** To reach Dempsey Hill, catch bus 7, 75, 77, 105, 106, 123 or 174 from behind Orchard MRT, on Orchard Blvd. Get off two stops after the Singapore Botanic Gardens, then walk up to your left. Buses 75 and 106 are two of several linking Holland Village with Dempsey Hill.

Top Sights
Singapore Botanic Gardens

For instant stress relief, take a dose of the Singapore Botanic Gardens. Suddenly the roar of traffic and 5.7 million voices melts into the branches, and the world is a tranquil, verdant paradise. At the tail end of Orchard Rd, Singapore's most famous sprawl of greenery offers more than just picnic-friendly lawns and lakes. It's home to ancient rainforest, themed gardens, unusual orchids and the occasional free concert. Breathe in, breathe out.

👁 Map p132, H3

📞 6471 7361

www.sbg.org.sg

1 Cluny Rd

garden admission free

🕑 5am–midnight

🚌 7, 75, 77, 105, 106, 123, 174,
Ⓜ Botanic Gardens

Male crimson sunbird perching on heliconia flower

Don't Miss

National Orchid Garden

The Botanic Gardens' now famous orchid breeding began in 1928 and you can get the historical low-down at the **National Orchid Garden** (adult/child under 12yr S\$5/free; ⏱8.30am-7pm, last entry 6pm). To date, its 3 hectares are home to over 1000 species and 2000 hybrids, around 600 of which are on display – the largest showcase of tropical orchids on Earth.

Rainforest

Older than the Botanic Gardens themselves, this precious patch of dense primeval rainforest offers a sample of the tree cover that once carpeted much of Singapore. Hit the rainforest boardwalk and surround yourself with 314 species of vegetation; over half are now considered rare in Singapore.

Ginger Garden

If you thought there was only one type of ginger, the compact Ginger Garden will set you straight. Located next to the National Orchid Garden, this 1-hectare space contains over 250 members of the Zingiberaceae family. It's also where you'll find ginger-centric restaurant Halia. A supporting cast of plants include the little-known Lowiaceae, with their orchid-like flowers.

Swan Lake

For lazy serenity and a touch of romanticism, it's hard to beat Swan Lake. One of three lakes in the Botanic Gardens, it's punctuated by a tiny island cluttered with nibong palms. Look out for the mute swans, imported all the way from Amsterdam.

☑ **Top Tips**

▸ Excellent, volunteer-run guided tours of the Botanic Gardens take place every Saturday. See the website for times and themes.

▸ Check the website for free opera concerts, occasionally held at the Botanic Gardens' Symphony Lake.

▸ Buy water when you see it, not when you need it: signage in the Botanic Gardens is not always consistent and backtracking is hardly fun, especially when you're thirsty.

✗ **Take a Break**

For a romantic nosh among the Botanic Garden's ginger plants, grab a table at Halia (p136).

Even more atmospheric is Indonesian restaurant Blue Bali (p135). Skirting the Botanical Gardens, its alfresco pavilions and cabanas look as though they're straight out of Ubud.

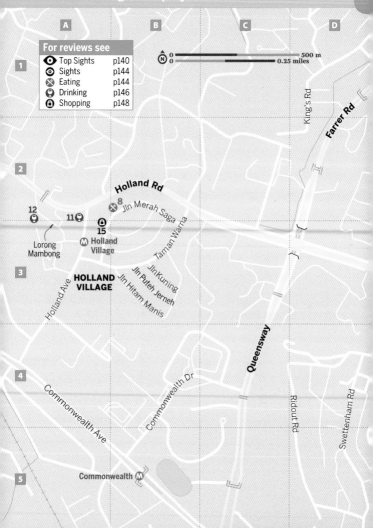

For reviews see

500 m
0.25 miles

King's Rd

Farrer Rd

Holland Rd

8

Jln Merah Saga

12

11

15

Taman Warna

Lorong Mambong

Holland Village

Jln Kuning

Jln Puteh Jerneh

Jln Hitam Manis

HOLLAND VILLAGE

Holland Ave

Queensway

Commonwealth Dr

Commonwealth Ave

Ridout Rd

Swettenham Rd

Commonwealth

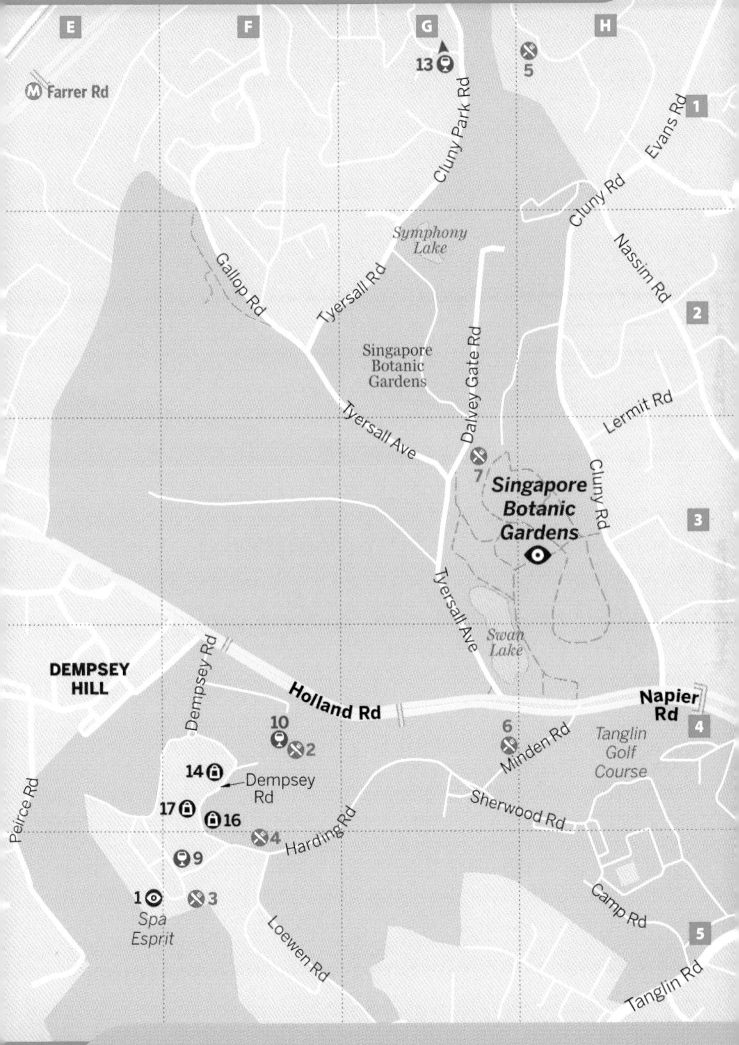

E

F

G

▶ 13 🍴

H

Ⓜ Farrer Rd

⊗ 5

Evans Rd

1

Cluny Park Rd

Cluny Rd

Nassim Rd

Symphony Lake

Gallop Rd

Tyersall Rd

Singapore Botanic Gardens

Dalvey Gate Rd

Lermit Rd

2

Tyersall Ave

⊗ 7

Singapore Botanic Gardens ◉

Cluny Rd

3

Tyersall Ave

Swan Lake

DEMPSEY HILL

Dempsey Rd

Holland Rd

Napier Rd

10 🍴
⊗ 2

14 🔒 ←Dempsey Rd

⊗ 6

Minden Rd

Tanglin Golf Course

4

17 🔒
🔒 16

Sherwood Rd

Peirce Rd

🍴 9

⊗ 4 Harding Rd

1 ◉
⊗ 3

Spa Esprit

Loewen Rd

Camp Rd

Tanglin Rd

5

CHOW MEIN WONG/GETTY IMAGES ©

Black pepper crab, a signature Singapore seafood dish

Sights

Spa Esprit   SPA

1  Map p132, E5

Spa Esprit is well known for its wide
range of pure essential oils. Try the
90-minute Back to Balance massage
to reboot your system or the fully organic Sink Your Skin Pear and Apple
Scrub for pure indulgence. You can
also customise body products to your
own taste. (☑6479 0070; www.spa-esprit.
com; 01-03, Block 8D, Beauty Emporium,
Dempsey Rd; ⊙10am-9pm; ☐7, 75, 77, 105,
106, 123, 174)

Eating

Long Beach Seafood   SEAFOOD $$$

2  Map p132, F4

One of Singapore's top seafood restaurant chains. Settle in on the verandah,
gaze out at the tropical greenery and
tackle the cult-status black-pepper crab.
The original Long Beach lays claim to
inventing the iconic dish, and the version here is fantastically peppery and
earthy. The kitchen is open later than
many restaurants in town. (☑6323 2222;
www.longbeachseafood.com.sg; 01-01, Block 25,
Dempsey Rd; mains S$14-48, crab per kilogram
around S$74; ⊙11am-3pm & 5pm-1am; ☐7, 75,
77, 105, 106, 123, 174)

Chopsuey

CHINESE $$$

3 🍴 Map p132, F5

Swirling ceiling fans, crackly 1930s tunes and ladies on rattan chairs – Chopsuey has colonial chic down pat. It serves revamped versions of retro American-Chinese dishes, but the real highlight is the lunchtime yum cha; standouts include Sichuan pepper-chilli tofu, pumpkin and cod dumplings, and *san choi bao* (minced meat in lettuce cups). The marble bar is perfect for solo diners. (📞9224 6611; www.chopsueycafe.com; 01-23, Block 10, Dempsey Rd; dumplings S$7-12, mains S$19-46; ⏰11.30am-midnight Mon-Fri, 10.30am-5pm & 6.30pm-midnight Sat & Sun; 🚌7, 75, 77, 105, 106, 123, 174)

PS Cafe

INTERNATIONAL $$

4 🍴 Map p132, F5

A chic, light-filled oasis of wooden floorboards, floor-to-ceiling windows and patio tables facing thick tropical foliage. From brunch to dinner, edibles are beautiful and healthy, whether it's fish-croquette Benedict or a 'Morocco miracle stack' of roasted portobello mushroom, grilled vegetables, smoked eggplant and couscous. No bookings taken for weekend brunch; head in at 9.30am to avoid the longest queues. (📞9070 8782; www.pscafe.com; 28B Harding Rd; mains S$26-34; ⏰11.30am-midnight Mon-Thu, 11.30am-2am Fri, 9.30am-2am Sat, 9.30am-midnight Sun; 🍴; 🚌7, 75, 77, 105, 106, 123, 174)

Blue Bali

INDONESIAN $$

5 🍴 Map p132, H1

Skirting the Botanic Gardens, Blue Bali is an enchanting dreamscape of Balinese wooden pavilions, cabanas over water and sarong-wrapped staff. Head in for a romantic sundowner and tapas-style bites like Javanese satay, fried homemade tofu or chilli-spiked pumpkin prawns, all of which better suit the low tables than the mains. (📞6733 0185; www.bluebali.sg; 1D Cluny Rd, Singapore Botanic Gardens; tapas S$8-20, mains S$16-32; ⏰4pm-midnight Tue-Fri, brunch 11am-3pm, 5pm-midnight Sat & Sun; 🛜🍴; 🚌7, 75, 77, 105, 106, 123, 174, Ⓜ Botanic Gardens)

Open Farm Community

INTERNATIONAL $$$

6 🍴 Map p132, G4

In a revamped greenhouse scattered with designer furniture and patronised by a health-conscious clientiele, Open Farm Community puts a tropical spin on the farm-to-table concept. Hand-picked herbs and vegetables from the garden lace a menu of clean, vibrant, comforting creations. From watercress soup to housemade pappardelle with mud crab, Thai curry sauce and coconut, dishes sing with intense, natural, life-affirming flavour. (📞6471 0306; www.openfarmcommunity.com; 130E Minden Rd; mains S$26-38; ⏰noon-10pm Mon-Fri, 11am-10pm Sat & Sun; 🚌7, 75, 77, 105, 106, 123, 174)

Halia

FUSION $$$

7 🍴 Map p132, G3

Atmospheric Halia is surrounded by the Botanic Gardens' ginger plants, a fact echoed in several unusual ginger-based dishes. Menus are a competent, fusion affair (think chilli-crab spaghettini), and the weekday set lunch (two/three courses S$28/32) is especially good value. There's a vegetarian and a kids' menu, and at weekends you can also do brunch (10am to 5pm); no reservations taken. (☏8444 1148; www.halia.com.sg; 1 Cluny Rd, Singapore Botanic Gardens; mains S$26-68; ◷noon-9.30pm Mon-Thu, to 10pm Fri, 10am-9.30pm Sun, to 10pm Sat; 🍴; 🚌7, 75, 77, 105, 106, 123, 174, ⓂBotanic Gardens)

Da Paolo Pizza Bar

ITALIAN $$

8 🍴 Map p132, B2

The successful Da Paolo chain has two outlets on this street alone: a deli-cafe (at No 43) and this polished bistro with terrace seating. Under a cowhide ceiling, svelte expats nosh on delicious thin-crust pizzas, competent pastas and warm chocolate brownie. There's a good-value weekday set lunch (S$23) and one-for-one happy hour noon to 2.30pm and 5.30pm to 7.30pm. (☏6479 6059; www.dapaolo.com.sg; 01-46, 44 Jln Merah Saga; pizzas S$20-31, pasta S$22-28; ◷noon-2.30pm & 5.30-10.30pm Mon-Fri, 11am-10.30pm Sat & Sun; ⓂHolland Village)

Q Local Life

Hit the Kitchen

Both novices and serious local foodies head to **Palate Sensations Cooking School** (Map p132; A5; ☏6478 9746; www.palatesensations.com; 01-03, Chromos, 10 Biopolis Rd; 3hr courses from S$100; ◷by appointment; ⓂBuona Vista) to hone their skills with top-notch chefs. Standard courses run for three hours and are wonderfully hands-on, spanning anything from Thai favourites to North Indian cuisine and French designer eclairs. For a true Singaporean culinary adventure, sign up for the tourist class to learn how to perfect local favourites like chilli crab and beef *rendang*.

Drinking

Green Door

BAR

9 🍷 Map p132, F5

Wide sky, sinuous palms and the odd frangipani breeze: slip behind the green gate for a little tropical seduction. Under gramophone lights, barkeeps shake and stir twisted classics (think Lillet Blanc–laced Negronis) splashed with herbs and fruit straight from the garden. Early-bird specials (5pm to 8pm Monday to Saturday, from 1pm Sunday) are decent, pulling in a languid expat crowd. (☏6479 5945; www.theprivegroup.com.sg/index.php/thegreendoor; Block 13A, Dempsey Rd; ◷5pm-midnight Mon-Thu, to 1.15am Fri & Sat, 1pm-midnight Sun; 🛜; 🚌7, 75, 77, 105, 106, 123, 174)

RedDot Brewhouse   MICROBREWERY

10 🍴 Map p132, F4

In a quiet spot in Dempsey Hill, RedDot has been pouring its own microbrews for years. Ditch the average food and focus on the suds, sipped to the sound of screeching parrots. There are eight beers on tap (from S$6.50 for a half-pint), including an eye-catching, spirulina-spiked green lager. Happy hour runs from noon to 7pm, with S$5 half-pints and S$9 pints. (☏ 6475 0500; www.reddotbrewhouse.com.sg; 01-01, Block 25A, Dempsey Rd; mains $20-36; ⏱ noon-midnight Mon-Thu, to 2am Fri & Sat, 10.30am-midnight Sun; 🚌 7, 75, 77, 105, 106, 123, 174)

Park   BAR

11 🍴 Map p132, A2

Industrial yellow tables, shophouse tiles and filament bulbs complete the hip fit-out of this converted-shipping-container bar. The outdoor patio seating and well-priced pints for this part of town ensure its popularity with locals and passers-by. Order a side of Spam chips (thinly sliced, deep-fried Spam), one of life's surprises. (☏ 9721 3815; www.parkgroup.com.sg; 01-01, 281 Holland Ave; ⏱ 11am-midnight Tue-Thu, to 2am Fri-Sun; 🛜; Ⓜ Holland Village)

Wala Wala Café Bar   BAR

12 🍴 Map p132, A2

Perennially packed at weekends (and most evenings, in fact), Wala Wala has live music on the 2nd floor, with

warm-up acts Monday to Friday from 7pm and main acts nightly from 9.30pm. Downstairs it pulls in football fans with its large sports screens. As at most nearby places, tables spill out onto the street in the evenings. (☏ 6462 4288; www.walawala.sg; 31 Lorong Mambong; ⏱ 4pm-1am Mon-Thu, 4pm-2am Fri, 3pm-2am Sat, 3pm-1am Sun; Ⓜ Holland Village)

Gastronomia

CAFE

13 🚇 Map p132, G1

Directly across the road from the Botanic Gardens MRT station, this casual coffeeshop is a perfect pit stop before or after your garden visit. Pull up a chair on the breezy verandah or grab a coffee to go and head upstairs to explore the trendy fashion and homewares boutiques geared towards the local expat community.

Local Life

A Virtuous Morning

If you feel like stretching your limbs, join the early morning fitness fanatics who descend on the Botanic Gardens (p130) from sunrise to stroll, run, roll out yoga mats and submit to bootcamp instructors. Keep an eye out for the mesmerising tai chi classes; the ones using the fans or swords are the best. You'll find plenty of shelters in case the heavens open, but water fountains are hard to locate, so best bring your own water bottle. Workout done, reward yourself with breakfast at **Casa Verde** (Map p133, H2; ☎6467 7326; www.casaverde.com.sg; 1 Cluny Rd, Singapore Botanic Gardens; lunch S\$9.50-19.50, pizza S\$24, dinner mains S\$18-35; ⏰7.30am-11pm; 🚌7, 75, 77, 105, 106, 123, 174, Ⓜ Botanic Gardens) at the Nassim Gate Visitors Centre, or Gastronomia, just outside the Bukit Timah gate, the latter conveniently situated next to the Botanic Gardens MRT.

(☎6468 7010; www.dapaolo.com.sg; Cluny Ct, 501 Bukit Timah Rd; ⏰7.30am-10pm; Ⓜ Botanic Gardens)

Shopping

Shang Antique

ANTIQUES

14 🔒 Map p132, F4

Specialising in antique religious artefacts from Cambodia, Laos, Thailand, India and Burma, as well as reproductions, Shang Antique has items dating back nearly 2000 years – with price tags to match. Those with more style than savings can pick up old opium pots, beautiful Thai silk scarves or Burmese ornamental rice baskets for under S\$40. (☎6388 8838; www.shangantique.com.sg; 01-03, Block 18D, Dempsey Rd; ⏰10.30am-6.30pm; 🚌7, 75, 77, 105, 106, 123, 174)

Bynd Artisan

ARTS & CRAFTS

15 🔒 Map p132, A3

Bespoke-stationery and leather connoisseurs will love this sublime store that prides itself on artisanal excellence. Select from the range of handmade journals or spend time customising your own. Other items to choose from include leather travel accessories and jewellery pieces. For the complete artist experience, sign up for a course in bookbinding, modern calligraphy or watercolour brushwork. (☎6475 1680; www.byndartisan.com; 01-54, 44 Jln Merah Saga; courses from S\$78;

Tai chi in the Botanic Gardens

⊘noon-9pm Mon-Fri, from 10am Sat & Sun;
Ⓜ Holland Village)

Em Gallery
FASHION, HOMEWARES

16 🔒 Map p132, F4

Singapore-based Japanese designer
Emiko Nakamura keeps Dempsey's
society ladies looking whimsically
chic in her light, sculptural creations. Emiko also collaborates with
hill tribes in northern Laos to create
naturally dyed handwoven handi-
crafts, such as bags and cushions.
Other homewares might include
limited-edition (and reasonably
priced) Khmer pottery from Cambodia. (✆6475 6941; www.emtradedesign.
com; 01-04/05, Block 16, Dempsey Rd;

⊘10am-7pm Mon-Fri, 11am-7pm Sat & Sun;
🚌7, 75, 77, 105, 106, 123, 174)

Pasardina Fine Living
ANTIQUES, HOMEWARES

17 🔒 Map p132, F4

If you plan on giving your home a
tropical Asian makeover, this rambling treasure trove is a good starting
point. Inspired by traditional Indonesian design, its collection includes
beautiful teak furniture, ceramic and
wooden statues, bark lampshades and
the odd wooden archway. (✆6472
0228; www.pasardina.com; 01-10, Block 13,
Demspey Rd; ⊘10am-6.30pm Mon-Fri, noon-
7pm Sat & Sun; 🚌7, 75, 77, 105, 106, 123, 174)

Explore

West & Southwest Singapore

Home to Singapore's epic container terminals, this corner of the city is often overlooked by visitors, who pass through only to take the cable car between Mt Faber and Sentosa. But look closer and you'll find some worthy magnets, among them the spectacular Southern Ridges trail, impressive art hubs Gillman Barracks and NUS Museum, as well as languid, colonial survivor Colbar.

The Sights in a Day

Enjoy a morning wander through **Labrador Nature Reserve** (p148), a sea-flanking pocket of green with shaded lawn and tropical forest scattered with wartime relics. Done, explore tranquil art-gallery complex **Gillman Barracks** (p147), kooky, old-school theme park **Haw Par Villa** (p147), or continue further on the MRT Yellow Line to Kent Ridge, from where a shuttle bus leads to the impressive **NUS Museum** (p146) and **Lee Kong Chian Natural History Museum** (p146).

Whichever option you choose, hop back on the MRT and get off at Pasir Panjang for cheap chow at **Eng Lock Koo** (p149). From here, amble up to hilltop **Reflections at Bukit Chandu** (p143) to wise up on the area's bloody past, then step inside adjoining Kent Ridge Park to begin your easy trek along the jungle-fringed **Southern Ridges** (p142) walking trail.

The walk terminates at Mt Faber, where drinks and bites are served with lofty views at family-friendly **Spuds & Aprons** (p150). Alternatively, catch a taxi to British colonial mess hall turned drinking hole **Colbar** (p150) or hip hawker hub and live-music venue **Timbre+** (p149).

◉ Top Sights

Southern Ridges (p142)

♥ Best of Singapore

Museums & Galleries
NUS Museum (p146)

Lee Kong Chian Natural History Museum (p146)

Gillman Barracks (p147)

Food
Tamarind Hill (p148)

Timbre+ (p149)

PeraMakan (p149)

For Kids
Haw Par Villa (p147)

Rink (p148)

Jurong East Swimming Complex (p148)

Getting There

Ⓜ **MRT** Southwest Singapore is well served by the MRT. Some attractions have their namesake stations. Otherwise, HarbourFront (Yellow and Purple Lines), Pasir Panjang (Yellow Line), Jurong East (Green and Red Lines) and Kent Ridge (Yellow Line) are useful.

Top Sights
Southern Ridges

A series of parks and hills connecting Mt Faber to West Coast Park, the Southern Ridges will have you trekking through the jungle without ever really leaving the city. While the whole route spans 9km, the best stretch is from Kent Ridge Park to Mt Faber. It's relatively easy, and serves up some stunning sights, from lofty skyline and jungle vistas to a seriously striking, wave-like walkway.

◉ Map p144, C3

www.nparks.gov.sg

Ⓜ Pasir Panjang

Don't Miss

Reflections at Bukit Chandu

Commemorating the last stand of the Malay Regiment against the Japanese in 1942, Reflections at Bukit Chandu combines first-hand accounts, personal artefacts and films to describe the brutal battle that almost wiped out the regiment.

Kent Ridge Park

Behind Reflections at Bukit Chandu you'll find Kent Ridge Park. It's strangely deserted so you'll have its short, yet wonderful, canopy walk pretty much to yourself. From here, stroll downhill to HortPark.

Forest Walk

A leaf-like bridge crosses over Alexandra Rd from HortPark, leading to the stunning Forest Walk. While you can opt for the Earth trail, the Elevated Walkway offers eye-level views of the jungle canopy covering Telok Blangah Hill.

Henderson Waves

The remarkable Henderson Waves (pictured), an undulating sculptural walkway suspended 36m above the forest floor, sits between Telok Blangah Hill Park and Mt Faber Park. The towers that seem to rise out of the jungle are part of Reflections at Keppel Bay – a residential development designed by renowned architect Daniel Libeskind.

Mt Faber

Stretching 105m above the southern fringe of the city, Mt Faber's terraced trails wind past strategically positioned viewpoints. It's here you'll find the cable-car service to HarbourFront and Sentosa.

☑ Top Tips

▶ The best time to hit the trail is late afternoon. You avoid the worst of the midday heat and can make it to Mt Faber in time for sunset drinks or dinner.

▶ Wear comfortable shoes, sunglasses and a hat. If rain is on the cards, bring an umbrella. And always pack plenty of water.

▶ Bring your camera. The walk delivers beautiful views of the city, jungle and South China Sea.

▶ If you encounter monkeys, do not feed them. This only encourages them to pester humans.

✗ Take a Break

For drinks and yakitori with stunning city views, head to Faber Bistro (p150). For more casual bites, opt for Spuds & Aprons (p150), also atop Mt Faber.

Kent Ridge Ⓜ **A**

National
University
of Singapore

1

ⵣ 9 **B**

Ayer Rajah Expwy (ADE)

Science Park Dr

Portsdown Rd

◉ 1, 2,
5, 7

🚻 13 **C**

Portsdown Ave

Queensway **D**

Buona Vista South Rd

Kent
Ridge
Park

2
◉ 4
◉ Haw Par
Villa

Haw Par
Villa Ⓜ

Buona Vista South Rd

Jln Mat Jambol

Hort
Park

Gillman
Barracks

3

Pasir Panjang Rd

Pasir
Panjang Ⓜ

Pepys Rd

❌ 11

◉ Southern
Ridges

West Coast Hwy

**PASIR
PANJANG**

Alexandra Rd

4

Ⓜ Labrador
Park

Labrador Villa Rd

Port Rd

❌ 8

5

Sebarok Channel

◉ 6
Labrador
Nature
Reserve

For reviews see

◉ Top Sights	p152
◉ Sights	p156
❌ Eating	p158
🍷 Drinking	p160
🛍 Shopping	p161

Ⓝ

0 ——————— 500 m
0 ——————— 0.25 miles

E F G H

1

Singapore River

Tiong Bahru Rd

Alexandra Rd

Ⓜ Redhill

Delta Stadium

Tiong Bahru Rd

Henderson Rd

Lower Delta Rd

Tiong Bahru Park

Ⓜ Tiong Bahru

2

Henderson Park

Jln Bukit Merah

Ayer Rajah Expwy (ADE)

Jln Bukit Merah

3

Telok Blangah Hill Park

Henderson Rd

4

Lower Delta Rd

❌12

Mt Faber Park

▲ Mt Faber

Telok Blangah Ⓜ

❌10

5

Telok Blangah Rd

HarbourFront Ⓜ

15 🔒

Sentosa Gateway

🏛14

VivoCity

Keppel Harbour

Pulau Keppel

HarbourFront Cruise & Ferry Terminal

SIVAKUMAR SATHIAMOORTHY/GETTY IMAGES ©

Haw Par Villa

Sights

NUS Museum

MUSEUM

1 ⊙ Map p144, A1

Located on the verdant campus of the National University of Singapore (NUS), this museum is one of the city's lesser-known cultural delights. Ancient Chinese ceramics and bronzes, as well as archaeological fragments found in Singapore, dominate the ground-floor Lee Kong Chian Collection; one floor up, the South and Southeast Asian Gallery showcases paintings, sculpture and textiles from the region. The Ng Eng Teng Collection is dedicated to Ng Eng Teng (1934–2001), Singapore's foremost modern artist, best known for his figurative sculptures. (☎6516 8817; www.nus.edu.sg/museum; University Cultural Centre, 50 Kent Ridge Cres; admission free; ⊙10am-7.30pm Tue-Fri, to 6pm Sat & Sun; Ⓜ Clementi, then bus 96)

Lee Kong Chian Natural History Museum

MUSEUM

2 ⊙ Map p144, A1

What looks like a giant rock bursting with greenery is actually Singapore's high-tech, child-friendly natural history museum. The main Biodiversity Gallery delves into the origin of life using a stimulating combo of fossils, taxidermy and interactive displays. Hard to miss are Prince, Apollonia and Twinky: three 150-million-year-old Diplodocidsauropod dinosaur skeletons, two with their original skulls. Upstairs, the Heritage Gallery explores the collection's 19th-century origins, with an interesting section on Singapore's geology to boot. (☑6601 3333; lkcnhm.nus.edu.sg; 2 Conservatory Dr; adult/child under 13yr S$21/12; ⏰10am-7pm Tue-Sun, last entry 5.30pm; Ⓜ Kent Ridge, then bus A2 (university shuttle)

Gillman Barracks   GALLERY

3 ◎ Map p144, D3

Built in 1936 as a British military encampment, Gillman Barracks is now a rambling art outpost with 11 galleries scattered around verdant grounds. Among these is New York's **Sundaram Tagore** (☑6694 3378; www.sundaramtagore.com; 01-05 Gillman Barracks; admission free; ⏰11am-7pm Tue-Sat, to 6pm Sun; Ⓜ Labrador Park), whose stable of artists includes award-winning photographers Edward Burtynsky and Annie Leibovitz.

Also on-site is the **NTU Centre for Contemporary Art** (☑6339 6503; www.ntu.ccasingapore.org; Block 43 Malan Rd, Gillman Barracks; admission free; ⏰noon-7pm Tue-Thu, Sat & Sun, to 9pm Fri; Ⓜ Labrador Park), a forward-thinking art-research centre hosting art talks, lectures and contemporary exhibitions from dynamic regional and international artists working in a variety of media.

To reach Gillman Barracks, catch the MRT to Labrador Park station and walk north up Alexandra Rd for 800m; the entry to Gillman Barracks is on your right. A one-way taxi fare from the CBD will set you back around S$10. (www.gillmanbarracks.com; 9 Lock Rd; admission free; ⏰11am-7pm Tue-Sat, to 6pm Sun; Ⓜ Labrador Park)

Haw Par Villa   MUSEUM, PARK

4 ◎ Map p144, A2

The refreshingly weird and kitsch Haw Par Villa was the brainchild of Aw Boon Haw, the creator of the medicinal salve Tiger Balm. After Aw Boon Haw built a villa here in 1937 for his beloved brother and business partner, Aw Boon Par, the siblings began building a Chinese-mythology theme park within the grounds. Top billing goes to the Ten Courts of Hell, a walk-through exhibit depicting the gruesome torments awaiting sinners in the underworld. (☑6872 2780; 262 Pasir Panjang Rd; admission free; ⏰9am-7pm, Ten Courts of Hell exhibit 9am-5.45pm; Ⓜ Haw Par Villa)

Tiger Brewery   BREWERY

5 ◎ Map p144, A1

You've been drinking its beers all holiday, so you might as well see how they make them. Visits to the Tiger Brewery are divided into two parts: the first is a 45-minute tour of the place, including the brewhouse and the packaging hall; the second is the real highlight – 45 minutes of free beer tasting in the wood-and-leather Tiger Tavern. Tours must be booked in advance. (☑6860 3005; www.tigerbrewery-tour.com.sg; 459 Jln Ahmad Ibrahim; adult/

Local Life
Making a Public Splash

Singapore has some seriously impressive public pools, which, at a couple of dollars or less, are among the island's best bargains. Top of the list is **Jurong East Swimming Complex** (6563 5052; 21 Jurong East St 31; weekdays/weekends S\$2/2.60; ⏱8am-9.30pm Tue, Thu, Fri & Sun, from 6.30am Wed & Sat; Ⓜ Chinese Garden), a wow-inducing combo of giant wave pool, lazy river, waterslides, wading pool, jacuzzi and Olympic-sized pool.

Expect huge crowds on weekends. The centre is a 600m walk from Chinese Garden MRT. Before heading in, double check opening times; visit www.myactivesg.com for more information.

child S\$18/12; ⏱1pm, 2pm, 3pm, 4pm & 5pm Mon-Sat; Ⓜ Joo Koon, then bus 182, 182M)

Labrador Nature Reserve   PARK

6 ◎ Map p144, D5

Combining forest trails rich in birdlife and a beachfront park, Labrador Park is scattered with evocative British war relics, only rediscovered in the 1980s. Look out for old gun emplacements mounted on moss-covered concrete casements, as well as for the remains of the entrance to the old fort that stood guard on this hill. The reserve's hilly terrain sweeps down to the shore, where expansive lawns, shade and the sound of lapping waves invite a lazy picnic. (www.nparks.gov.sg; Labrador Villa Rd; ⏱24hr; 🚌408, Ⓜ Labrador Park)

Rink   SKATING

7 ◎ Map p144, A1

Singapore's first Olympic-sized ice rink is located on level three of youthful mall JCube. Between 9.45pm and 11.45pm on Fridays and Saturdays, disco bunnies get their skates on for the weekly 'Disco on Ice'. (6684 2374; www.therink.sg; Level 3, JCube, 2 Jurong East Central 1; adult/child S\$14/12, with hire of skate boots, gloves & socks S\$21.50/19.50; ⏱public skating times vary; Ⓜ Jurong East)

Eating

Tamarind Hill   THAI \$\$\$

8 ✕ Map p144, D4

In a colonial bungalow in Labrador Park, Tamarind Hill sets an elegant scene for exceptional Thai. The highlight is Sunday brunch (noon to 3pm), which offers a buffet of beautiful cold dishes and salads, as well as the ability to order as many dishes off the à la carte menu as you like (the sautéed squid is sublime). Book ahead. (6278 6364; www.tamarindrestaurants.com; 30 Labrador Villa Rd; mains S\$18-59, Sun brunch S\$60; ⏱noon-2.30pm & 6.30-10.30pm; 🛜; 🚌408 (weekends only), Ⓜ Labrador Park)

Timbre+

HAWKER $

9 🍴 Map p144, B1

Welcome to the new generation of hawker centres. With over 30 food outlets, Timbre+ has it all: artwork-covered shipping containers, Airstream trailer food trucks, craft beer, live music Monday to Saturday nights (from 8pm), and the list goes on. But it's the food that draws the crowds: a mixture of traditional and new age. Head here in the late afternoon before the old-school hawker stalls shut at 6pm. (www.timbre-plus.sg; JTC LaunchPad@one-north, 73A Ayer Rajah Cres; dishes from S$3; ⏰6am-midnight Mon-Thu, to 1am Fri & Sat; Ⓜ️One North)

PeraMakan

PERANAKAN $$

10 🍴 Map p144, E5

Run by a genial couple of cooking enthusiasts, this paragon of homestyle Baba-Nonya cuisine migrated from its spiritual Joo Chiat home. Thankfully, classics such as *sambal* squid and *rendang* (spicy coconut curry) remain as plate-lickingly good as ever. One dish definitely not worth missing is the *ayam buah keluak* (chicken in a rich spicy sauce served with Indonesian black-nut pulp). (📞6377 2829; www.peramakan.com; L3 Keppel Club, 10 Bukit Chermin Rd; mains S$14-28; ⏰11.30am-2pm & 6-9pm; 📶📶; Ⓜ️Telok Blangah)

Eng Lock Koo

HAWKER $

11 🍴 Map p144, C3

Handy for breakfast or lunch if you're on your way to either Reflec-tions at Bukit Chandu or Kent Ridge Park for the Southern Ridges walk, this small collection of stalls inside an airy corner shop premises does tea and coffee, not to mention hawker favourites such as chicken rice and *nasi goreng* (fried rice). (114 Pasir Panjang Rd, cnr Pepys Rd; mains from S$3; ⏰individual stalls vary, generally 5am-3pm; Ⓜ️Pasir Panjang)

Masons

INTERNATIONAL $$

Located on the grounds of Gillman Barracks (see 3 🔘 Map p144, D3), this handy cafe-bistro comes with high

🔍 Local Life
Kranji Farms

For a refreshingly different take on Singaporean life, consider visiting Singapore's small, thriving cluster of farms. A daily minibus service, the Kranji Express (Kranji MRT Station; adult/child $3/1, 9am to 6pm, every 75 minutes), does a loop from the Kranji MRT station, visiting many of the best farms en route.

One of the best is **Bollywood Veggies** (📞6898 5001; www.bollywoodveggies.com; 100 Neo Tiew Rd; admission S$2, Kranji Express passengers free; ⏰9.30am-6.30pm Wed-Fri, from 8am Sat & Sun; Ⓜ️Kranji, then Kranji Countryside Express bus), where you can ramble through rustic gardens planted with cashew, papaya and starfruit trees, and nosh on beautiful, healthy grub at the bistro.

ceilings, elegant verandah seating, and a marble bar with black leather sofas for a post-gallery cocktail (happy hour 4pm to 7pm). Italian flavours dominate the menu, with American staples including Bourbon-smoked ribs and a juicy beef burger. Herbivores and the health-conscious will appreciate the dedicated low-calorie and vegetarian options. (☑ 6694 2216; www.masons.sg; 01-17 Gillman Barracks, 9 Lock Rd; pizzas S$21-28, mains S$24-38; ◷ noon-11pm Mon-Sat, to 10pm Sun; ☑; Ⓜ Labrador Park)

Faber Peak
12 ✕ Map p144, G4   INTERNATIONAL $$

Faber Peak is the highest landing point of the cable-car line. In the terminal you'll find super-casual,

> ### Local Life
> #### Singapore Turf Club
> Although not quite as manic as the Hong Kong races, a trip to **Singapore Turf Club** (☑ 65-6879 1715; www.turfclub.com.sg; 1 Turf Club Ave; Level 1 Grandstand & Level 2 Gallop S$6, Owners' Lounge S$30; Ⓜ Kranji) is nevertheless a hugely popular day out (bring your passport). Races usually run on Fridays (6.20pm to 10.50pm) and Sundays (12.50pm to 6.30pm) and a dress code is enforced: no jogging shorts or singlets in the public grandstand; no shorts, collarless T-shirts or sandals in the Owners' Lounge.

family-friendly **Spuds & Aprons** (☑ 6377 9688; www.faberpeaksingapore.com; 109 Mt Faber Rd; mains S$14-38; ◷ 11am-10pm; Ⓜ HarbourFront), offering a mix of pastas, salads, and mains such as crispy pork belly and barbecue ribs. Outside **Faber Bistro** (☑ 6377 9688; www.mountfaber.com.sg; 101 Mt Faber Rd; mains S$15-38; ◷ 4-11pm Mon-Thu, to 2am Fri & Sat, 11am-11pm Sun; Ⓜ HarbourFront, cable car Mt Faber) offers hearty dishes, such as burgers and pizza, as well as patio dining.

The easiest way to get here is by taxi or cable car; the only other option is to walk. (☑ 6377 9688; www.faberpeak-singapore.com; 109 Mt Faber Rd; Ⓜ Harbour-Front, cable car Mt Faber)

Drinking

Colbar
13 🍺 Map p144, C1   BAR

Raffish Colbar is an evocative colonial throwback, a former British officers' mess turned languid drinking spot. It's still 1930-something here: a place where money is kept in a drawer, football team photos hang on the wall and locals linger with beers and well-priced ciders on the spacious verandah. It is still run by Mr and Mrs Lim, who opened the doors in 1953. (☑ 6779 4859; 9A Whitchurch Rd; ◷ 11am-midnight Tue-Sun, kitchen closes 8.30pm; Ⓜ Buona Vista, then bus 191)

SUHAIMI ABDULLAH/GETTY IMAGES ©

Shoppers at VivoCity mall

Privé

BAR

14 Map p144, F5

Located on an island out in the middle of Keppel Harbour, with the city on one side and Sentosa on the other, you really couldn't ask for a better location for evening drinks. You can expect to find an affluent, well-dressed crowd here, with guest DJs and occasional live music. The attached restaurant serves French-American cuisine and the all-day cafe offers tasty pastas, pizzas and burgers. (☎6776 0777; www.prive.com. sg; Keppel Bay Dr; ⏱5-11.30pm Mon-Thu, 5pm-12.30am Fri, noon-12.30am Sat, noon-midnight Sun; ⓜHarbourFront, then taxi)

Shopping

VivoCity

MALL

15 Map p144, H5

More than just Singapore's largest shopping mall, VivoCity offers that rare commodity: open space. There's an outdoor kids' playground on level two and a rooftop 'skypark' with free-to-use paddling pools. The retail mix is predominantly midrange, and there's a large Golden Village cineplex. (☎6377 6860; www.vivocity.com.sg; 1 HarbourFront Walk; ⏱10am-10pm; 🛜; ⓜHarbourFront, Sentosa Express)

The Best of
Singapore

Gardens by the Bay (p26)
BIGBOOM/SHUTTERSTOCK ©

Best Walks
Colonial Singapore

🏃 The Walk

In a city firmly fixed on the future, the Colonial District offers a rare, precious glimpse of a romanticised era and its architectural legacies. This is the Singapore of far-flung missionaries and churches, Palladian-inspired buildings, high-society cricket clubs and the legendary Raffles Hotel. This walk takes in some of the city's most beautiful heritage buildings, swaths of soothing greenery, spectacular skyline views and even a spot of contemporary Asian art. Time it to coincide with a postwalk lunch or dinner by the Singapore River.

Start Armenian Church; Ⓜ City Hall

Finish Old Hill Street Police Station; Ⓜ Clarke Quay

Length 2.6km; three to four hours with stops

✕ Take a Break

End your saunter with trademark chilli crab at **Jumbo Seafood** (p38).

Victoria Theatre Concert Hall

SAIKO3P/GETTY IMAGES ©

❶ Singapore Art Museum

The **Singapore Art Museum** (p32) occupies a former Catholic boys school. Original features include the shuttered windows, ceramic floor tiles and inner quadrangle. The central dome and arcade portico were early-20th-century additions.

❷ Raffles Hotel

Head southeast along Bras Basah Rd, passing the Renaissance-inspired Cathedral of the Good Shepherd, and the English Gothic CHIJMES, a convent turned-restaurant complex. Diagonally opposite CHIJMES is the legendary **Raffles Hotel** (p33).

❸ St Andrew's

You'll find wedding-cake **St Andrew's Cathedral** (p34) further south on North Bridge Rd. Completed in 1838, it was torn down after being struck by lightning (twice!), and rebuilt by Indian convicts in 1862. It's one of Singapore's few surviving examples of English Gothic architecture.

4 City Hall

Built in 1928, City Hall is where Lord Louis Mountbatten announced the Japanese surrender in 1945 and Lee Kuan Yew declared Singapore's independence in 1965. City Hall and the Old Supreme Court, built in 1939, now house the **National Gallery Singapore** (p24).

5 Padang

Opposite City Hall is the open field of the Padang, home to the Singapore Cricket Club and Singapore Recreation Club. It was here that the invading Japanese herded the European community together before marching them off to Changi Prison.

6 Victoria Theatre

Below where St Andrew's Rd curves to the left stand a group of colonial-era buildings, including the Victoria Theatre & Concert Hall. Completed in 1862, it was originally the Town Hall. It was also one of Singapore's first Victorian Revivalist buildings.

7 Old Hill Street Police Station

Hang a right to hit the Singapore River. The multicoloured building on the corner of Hill St is the **Old Hill Street Police Station**. Dubbed a 'skyscraper' when built in 1934, it's now home to a string of private contemporary art galleries.

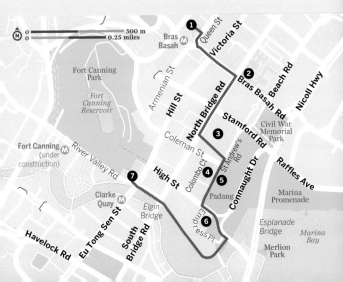

Best Walks
New-Millennium Singapore

🏃 The Walk

Singapore is not marching towards the future – it is inventing it. Drunk on ambition, the city has been diligently revamping itself with a bold new wave of quirky, edgy and sometimes controversial developments. This walk will see you exploring the very heart of the 'new Singapore', Marina Bay, a daring precinct where cultural buildings echo fruits and flowers, where bridges recall DNA strings, and where botanic gardens look straight off the set of *The Day of the Triffids*. Welcome to tomorrow.

Start Esplanade – Theatres on the Bay; Ⓜ Esplanade

Finish Gardens by the Bay; Ⓜ Bayfront

Length 2km; three hours with stops

🍴 Take a Break

End your time travel with street-food classics at breezy, easy hawker centre **Satay by the Bay** (p38).

SENG CHYE TEO/GETTY IMAGES ©

Gardens by the Bay

❶ Esplanade – Theatres on the Bay

Singapore's head-turning **Esplanade – Theatres on the Bay** (p43) houses a theatre and concert hall under two super structures of double-glazed laminated glass and aluminium sun-shades. Designed by Singapore's DP Architects and London's Michael Wilford & Partners, its price tag was a cool S$600 million. Head up to the rooftop garden for an applause-worthy view.

❷ Helix Bridge

Walk east along Marina Promenade to the 280m-long **Helix Bridge**. It's the world's first double-helix bridge, designed by Australia's Cox Architecture and Singapore's Architects 61. Viewing platforms offer an impressive vantage point for photos across to Collyer Quay, Merlion and Fullerton buildings.

❸ ArtScience Museum

The white, lotus-like building on the other side of the bridge is the

ArtScience Museum (p34). Opened in 2011, the structure is the work of Israeli-born architect Moshe Safdie. The building consists of 10 finger-like elements capped by skylights, lighting the galleries within. Beside the museum is the world's first floating Louis Vuitton store.

❹ Marina Bay Sands

Both the ArtScience Museum and the Louis Vuitton store form part of the ambitious Marina Bay Sands integrated resort, home to the lavish **Shoppes at Marina Bay Sands** (p47) and a gravity-defying cantilevered skydeck. Known as the 'SkyPark', the deck is large enough to park four-and-a-half A380s. Catch the lift to **CÉ LA VI SkyBar** (p34) for a blockbuster vista that is especially impressive on a clear day.

❺ Gardens by the Bay

From Marina Bay Sands, a pedestrian overpass leads you to **Gardens by the Bay** (p26), a new-millennium park housing the world's largest conservatories, an aerial walkway and state-of-the-art Supertrees whose trunks contain solar hot water and photovoltaic collectors, rainwater harvesting devices and venting ducts.

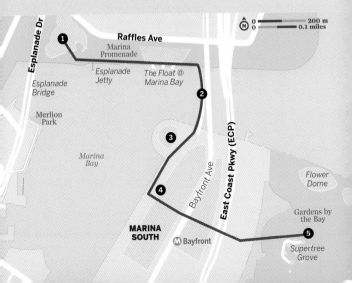

Best
Tours

Best Neighbourhood Tours

Original Singapore Walks (www.singapore-walks.com) Knowledgeable on-foot excursions through Chinatown, Little India, Kampong Glam, the Colonial District, Boat Quay, Haw Par Villa and war-related sites. Most tours do not require a booking; simply check the website for meeting times and places.

Chinatown Trishaw Night Tour (www.viator.com) An atmospheric, four-hour tour of Chinatown including dinner, on-foot exploration, a trishaw ride, and a bumboat cruise along the Singapore River. Hotel pick-ups and drop-offs are provided.

Trishaw Uncle (www.trishawuncle.com.sg) Hop on a trishaw for an old-fashioned ride through Bugis and Little India. The 45-minute tour also takes in the Singapore River. You'll find the trishaw terminal on Queen St, between the Fu Lu Shou Complex and Albert Centre Market and Food Centre.

Best River Tours

Singapore Ducktours (www.ducktours.com.sg) Informative, one-hour, land-and-water tours on a remodelled WWII amphibious Vietnamese war craft. The route focuses on Marina Bay and the Colonial District. The ticket kiosk and departure point is in Tower 5 of Suntec City, directly facing the Nicoll Hwy.

Singapore River Cruise (www.rivercruise.com.sg) Forty-minute bumboat river cruises that ply the stretch between the Quays and Marina Bay. Departure points include Clarke Quay, Raffles Landing and Boat Quay. The running commentary is a little cringe-inducing, but the trip itself is relaxing, with spectacular city views.

Best Themed Tours

Real Singapore Tours Insider tours (www.betelbox.com/singaporetours.htm) led by Tony Tan and the

ENTIENOU/GETTY IMAGES ©

team at Betel Box hostel. Choose from nature walks, coastline cycling or a Joo Chiat neighbourhood food odyssey (usually 6pm on Thursday).

Geraldene's Tours (www.geraldenestours.com) Offering a wealth of information, Singapore-born Geraldene has been conducting Singapore walking tours for more than 40 years. Her various private tours lend a unique insight into Singapore's history, architecture, religions, botany and culture. (p55)

Bukit Brown Tour (www.bukitbrown.com) Fascinating walking tours through one of Singapore's most historic, wild and beautiful cemeteries, currently under threat from development.

Best
Festivals

Best Hindu Festivals

Thaipusam (February) Kavadis (heavy metal frames) pierce parading devotees.

Deepavali (October) Little India glows for the 'Festival of Lights'.

Thimithi (November) Hindus walk over white hot coals at Sri Mariamman Temple.

Best Music Festivals

St Jerome's Laneway Festival (singapore. lanewayfestival.com) Uber-hip one-day indie music fest; January.

Singapore International Jazz Festival (www.sing-jazz.com) Three-day showcase of established and emerging jazz talent; March.

Mosaic Music Festival (www.mosaicmusicfestival. com) Ten days of world music, jazz and indie acts; March.

Singapore International Festival of Arts (www. sifa.sg) Small, world-class

offering of dance, drama and music; August and September.

ZoukOut (www.zoukout. com) Singapore's biggest outdoor dance party, held over two nights on Sentosa and featuring A-list international DJs; December.

Best Chinese Festivals

Chinese New Year (February) Dragon dances, fireworks, food and spectacular street decorations.

Hungry Ghost Festival (August) Fires, food and Chinese opera honour roaming spirits.

Mid-Autumn Festival (August/September) Lanterns light up Chinatown as revellers nibble on mooncakes. Takes place on the full moon of the eighth lunar month.

Best for Foodies

Singapore Food Festival (www.yoursingapore. com) Two weeks of tastings, special dinners and food-themed tours; July.

MICHAEL COYNE/GETTY IMAGES ©

World Gourmet Summit (www.worldgourmetsummit.com) Ten days of top chefs, master classes, workshops and lavish dinners; March/April.

Best Only-in-Singapore Festivals

Chingay (www.chingay.org. sg) Singapore's biggest street party, held on the 22nd day after Chinese New Year; February.

Singapore National Day (www.ndp.org.sg) Extravagant processions and fireworks. Snap tickets up well in advance; 9 August.

Formula One Night Race (www.singapore-f1-grand-prix.com) After-dark F1 racing on a spectacular Marina Bay street circuit; September.

Best
Shopping

Bangkok and Hong Kong might upstage it on the bargain front, but when it comes to choice, few cities match Singapore. Whether you're after Gucci mules, fashion-forward local threads or a 16th-century temple artefact, you'll have little trouble bagging it in Singapore's decadent malls, progressive boutiques and cluttered heirloom businesses.

Retail Roadmap

While mall-heavy Orchard Rd is Singapore's retail queen, it's only one of several retail hubs. For electronics, hit tech mall Sim Lim Square. Good places for antiques include Tanglin Shopping Centre, Dempsey Hill and Chinatown. For fabrics and textiles, scour Little India and Kampong Glam, the latter also known for perfume traders and indie-cool Haji Lane. For independent fashion, design and books, explore Tiong Bahru.

Bagging a Bargain

While Singapore is no longer a cut-price electronics nirvana, it can offer savings. Know the price of things beforehand, then browse and compare. Ask vendors what they can do to sweeten the deal; at the very least, they should be able to throw in a camera case or memory cards. Sim Lim Square mall is known for its range and negotiable prices, though it's also known for taking the uninitiated for a ride, not to mention for occasionally selling 'new' equipment that isn't quite new: a quick internet search will bring up blacklisted businesses. The best deals are on computers and cameras, with prices often 20% lower than major stores.

HEINRICH VAN DEN BERG/GETTY IMAGES ©

☑ **Top Tip**

▶ The Great Singapore Sale (www.greatsingaporesale.com.sg) delivers 10 weeks of sales from early June to mid-August. The best bargains are usually in the first week.

Best Souvenirs

Raffles Hotel Gift Shop
Everything from vintage poster prints to tea and tomes. (p45)

Antiques of the Orient
Beautiful old maps, prints and photos of Singapore and the region. (p59)

Naiise Design-literate Singaporean trinkets and homewares. (p45)

National Gallery Singapore The museum store stocks tasteful, design-

Pagoda St, Chinatown

savvy gifts, including specially commissioned pieces. (p24)

Best Luxury Malls

ION Orchard Mall A-list boutiques in Singapore's most impressive consumer temple. (p59)

Shoppes at Marina Bay Sands Bayside luxury and the world's first floating Louis Vuitton store. (p47)

Paragon Polished brands and a dedicated children's floor in the heart of Orchard Rd. (p59)

Best Midrange Malls

313@Somerset High Street staples and an upbeat vibe (Map p51, E4; www.313somerset.com.sg; 313 Orchard Rd; Ⓜ Somerset)

ION Orchard Mall ION's lower levels are dedicated to midrange fashion and accessories. (p59)

VivoCity Accessible labels galore at Singapore's biggest mall, just across from Sentosa. (p151)

Best for Design

Kapok Innovative threads and lifestyle objects at the National Design Centre. (p45)

Strangelets Eclectic homewares, accessories and more in on-trend Tiong Bahru. (p63)

Supermama Contemporary designer pieces with a Singaporean theme. (p110)

Bynd Artisan Handmade journals, leather travel accessories and jewellery. (p138)

Best Art & Antiques

Tanglin Shopping Centre Quality Asian antiques and art in a mall off Orchard Rd. (p59)

Utterly Art Affordable contemporary Southeast Asian art in a tiny Chinatown gallery. (p83)

Shang Antique Evocative temple artefacts and vintage Asian knick-knacks in Dempsey Hill. (p138)

Best for Tech

Sim Lim Square Six levels of laptops, cameras and more at Singapore's biggest tech mall. (p113)

Mustafa Centre No shortage of electronic gizmos, available 24 hours a day. (p113)

Best
Street Food

It's one of Singapore's great pleasures: ambling into a lively hawker centre in your flip-flops, navigating the steam, smoke and chatter of the stalls, then kicking back with a cold beer and a dirt-cheap feast of mouth-watering regional dishes. And the thrifty feasting doesn't end there, with enough old-school *kopitiams* (coffeeshops) and foodie-approved food courts to keep both tastebuds and wallets purring.

TRAVEL INK/GETTY IMAGES ©

Same, Same, but Different

Hawker centres, food courts and *kopitiams*: what's the difference? Hawker centres are usually stand-alone, open-air (or at least open-sided) structures with a raucous vibe and rows of food stalls peddling various local cuisines. Often found in malls, food courts are basically air-conditioned hawker centres with marginally higher prices, while coffeeshops, also called *kopitiams* (*tiam* is Hokkien for 'shop'), are open shopfront cafes, usually with a handful of stalls and roaming 'aunties' or 'uncles' taking drinks orders.

Hawker Etiquette

You're at a hawker centre. Now what? Bag a seat first, especially if it's busy. Sit a member of your group at a table, or lay a packet of tissues on a seat. Don't worry if there are no free tables; it's normal to share with strangers. If there's a table number, note it as the stall owner uses it as reference for food delivery. If the stall has a 'self service' sign, you'll have to carry the food to the table yourself. Otherwise, the vendor brings your order to you. Lastly, ignore wandering touts who try to sit you down and plonk menus in front of you.

Best Hawker Grub

Gluttons Bay Delicious hawker classics in an easy-to-navigate setting on Marina Bay. (p37)

Maxwell Food Centre One of Singapore's most tourist-friendly hawker centres on the cusp of Chinatown. (p75)

Chinatown Complex The loud, crowded hardcore hawker experience slap bang in central Chinatown. (p76)

Timbre+ A next-gen hawker hub with food trucks, craft suds and live tunes in the island's southwest. (p149)

Lau Pa Sat Worth a visit for its magnificent wrought-iron architecture alone. (p78)

Food court noodles

Best Food Courts

Takashimaya Food Village Basement wonderland of Japanese, Korean and other Asian delicacies on Orchard Rd. (p60)

Food Republic Hawker-style classics and restaurant-style nooks atop an Orchard Rd mall. (p56)

Rasapura Masters Street food from Asia and beyond inside ostentatious Marina Bay Sands. (Map p31, G4; 📞6506 0161; www.rasapura.com.sg; B2-50, The Shoppes at Marina Bay Sands, 2 Bayfront Ave; dishes from S$6; ⏰food court 24hr, stall hours vary; 🛜; Ⓜ Bayfront)

Best Kopitiams

Ya Kun Kaya Toast Historic hang-out serving Singapore's best runny eggs and *kaya* (coconut jam) toast in the CBD. (p78)

Killiney Kopitiam Another top spot for old-school Singaporean breakfasts, plus solid curries, laksa and *nasi lemak* (coconut rice served with fried ikan bilis, peanuts and a curry dish) off Orchard Rd. (p55)

Coffee Break Singaporean *kopi* (coffee) gets a modern makeover at this low-key drink stall in Chinatown. (p69)

Best Malay

Zam Zam Old-school *murtabak* (stuffed savoury pancake) in the shadow of Sultan Mosque. (p103)

Warong Nasi Pariaman A much-loved, no-frills *nasi padang* (rice with curries) joint in Kampong Glam. (p104)

Malaysian Food Street Sentosa's indoor hawker centre features some of Malaysia's most popular street-food vendors. (p122)

Satay Street Sizzling, skewers on a blocked-off CBD street behind La Pau Sat. (p78)

Best Indian

Bismillah Biryani Hands down the best darn biryani in Singapore. (p104)

Tekka Centre Little India's take on the bustling hawker centre. (p103)

Moghul Sweets A cult-status stall selling subcontinental sweets in Little India. (p106)

Best
Dining

Beyond the cheap, wham-bam thrills of hawker centres and food courts is a vibrant scene of lauded restaurants in both the midrange and top-end categories. Options are endless: Japanese fusion in an Orchard Rd mall, elegant Italian in a colonial bungalow, even prized French and Peranakan in a blockbuster art gallery.

TATYANA KILDISHEVA/GETTY IMAGES ©

An Evolving Scene

Singapore's restaurant scene is booming. From celebrated local chef Violet Oon's National Kitchen by Violet Oon to hot Australian chef Sam Aisbett's Whitegrass, the city has an ever-expanding legion of top-notch, celebrity-chef nosheries. Iggy's remains one of Asia's most coveted destination restaurants, with French chef Julien Royer's new offering Odette providing lofty competition. Most exciting is Singapore's new breed of midrange eateries, which deliver sharp, produce-driven menus in an altogether more relaxed setting. Among the best are Australian grill Burnt Ends and Japanese *izakaya* Neon Pigeon, two of a string of newcomers that have transformed Chinatown and Keong Saik into dining 'it' spots.

Food Blogs

For local foodie opinions, check out some of Singapore's top food bloggers. On-the-ball Leslie Tay reviews mainly hawker food around the island at ieatishootipost.sg, while food show radio presenter Daniel Ang loves talking about, eating and sharing food at www.danielfooddiary.com. Lady Ironchef (actually a bloke) offers highly respected opinions and helpful 'best lists' on his site www.ladyironchef.com, while Seth scours the island for the best fare at www.sethlui.com.

☑ **Top Tip**

▶ Tipping is unnecessary in Singapore, as most restaurants impose a 10% service charge – and nobody ever tips in hawker centres. That said, many do leave a discretionary tip for superlative service at higher-end restaurants.

Best Celeb-Chef Hot Spots

Odette Modern French from Gallic superstar Julien Royer. (p36)

National Kitchen by Violet Oon Sensational Straits cuisine from the Julia Childs of Singapore. (p36)

Iggy's Japanese ingredients meet global influences in the kitchen of Masahiro Isono. (p53)

Whitegrass Antipodean produce meets Asian inspiration at Aussie Sam Aisbett's fine-dining darling. (p36)

Burnt Ends Extraordinary barbecued meats from West Australian expat Dave Pynt. (p74)

Best Crab

Momma Kong's Good deals, huge buns and Singapore's freshest Sri Lankan crabs. (p74)

Long Beach Seafood Cult-status black-pepper crab in an old Dempsey barracks. (p134)

No Signboard Seafood Superlative white-pepper crab in red-light Geylang. (p89)

Best Date Spots

Il Lido at the Cliff Italian flavours in a sultry, discreet Sentosa location. (p121)

Buona Terra Authentic, high-end regional Italian off Orchard Rd. (p53)

Pollen Innovative, sophisticated Euro-Asian dishes in a space-age Flower Dome. (p37)

Best Fusion & Western

Gordon Grill Carnivorous highs and a nostalgic air off Orchard Rd. (p54)

Kilo Orchard Japanese fusion It-kid in an Orchard Rd mall. (p55)

Neon Pigeon Japanese *izakaya* share plates in dining epicentre Keong Saik (Map p70, B4; ☎65-6222 3623; www.neon-pigeonsg.com; 1 Keong Saik Rd; small dishes S$8-20, large dishes S$14-38; ◷6-11pm Mon-Thu, to 11.30pm Fri & Sat; ☎; Ⓜ Outram Park, Chinatown)

Super Loco Riverside Mexican street food and party vibe to match. (p38)

Best Brunch

Knolls High-end buffet, free-flow drinks and strutting peacocks on Sentosa. (p122)

Tamarind Hill Exquisite Sunday Thai in a jungle-like setting. (p148)

PS Cafe Beautiful produce, lunching ladies and a tropical-chic vibe in Dempsey. (p135)

Best Peranakan & Chinese

National Kitchen by Violet Oon Lauded Peranakan at the National Gallery Singapore. (p36)

Paradise Dynasty Superlative dumplings and hand-pulled noodles. (p54)

Song Fa Bak Kut Teh Steamy pork-rib soul soup. (p38)

PeraMakan Spicy Peranakan in a resort-like setting in the southwest. (p149)

Best Indian & Indonesian

Curry Culture Nuanced Indian flavours in a smart-casual setting in Robertson Quay. (p38)

Lagnaa Barefoot Dining Flexible spice levels in Little India. (p103)

Blue Bali Finger-licking Indonesian bites in a tropical setting. (p135)

Tambuah Mas Authentic, made-from-scratch Indonesian on Orchard Rd. (p54)

Best Retro Singapore

Colbar Hainanese-style Western classics in a former officers mess in the southwest. (p150)

Best
For Kids

SHIRLYN LOO/GETTY IMAGES ©

Safe, respectable, reliable Singapore would make an admirable babysitter. From interactive museum galleries and tactile animal sanctuaries to an island packed with blockbuster theme-park thrills, young ones are rarely an afterthought. Hotels supply cots, most cafes will have highchairs and modern malls have family rooms in which to feed a baby and change nappies. If you're after a little quality family time, Southeast Asia's Little Red Dot has you covered.

Sentosa: Pleasure Island

While kid-friendly attractions are spread out across Singapore, you'll find the greatest concentration on the island of Sentosa. Here you'll find the LA-style Universal Studios theme park, plus a long list of supporting attractions, from the ambitious SEA Aquarium to zip-lining and Segway tours. You'll need at least a full day to experience everything Sentosa has to offer, not to mention a well-stocked wallet, as most activities, rides and shows cost extra.

Discounts

Kids receive up to 50% discount at most tourist venues. Those aged six years and under enjoy free entry to many of Singapore's top museums, including the National Gallery Singapore, National Museum of Singapore, Asian Civilisations Museum and Peranakan Museum. Kids under 0.9m tall can ride the MRT for free. Full-time students with photo ID cards also enjoy discounts at many attractions.

☑ **Top Tip**

▶ Large attractions often have strollers for hire. Somewhat frustrating, however, is the requirement to fold strollers before boarding buses; the MRT allows you to wheel straight on.

Best Museums

National Museum of Singapore An evocative exploration of Singaporean history and culture, with audio-visual displays, artefacts and child-friendly signs. (p28)

National Gallery Singapore Blockbuster art museum with a dedicated kids' art facility and vibrant youth programs running throughout the year. (p24)

ArtScience Museum Temporary, world-class art and science exhibitions with interactive kids' programs. (p34)

Lee Kong Chian Natural History Museum Engaging exhibits, complete with giant dinosaurs and fantastical displays of exotic beasts from both land and sea. (p146)

MINT Museum of Toys A jaw-dropping, Technicolor collection of over 50,000 rare, collectable toys from around the globe. (p35)

Best Thrills & Spills

Universal Studios Hollywood-inspired rides, roller coasters and shows for the young and young-at-heart. (p116)

iFly Plummet a virtual 2743m without a plane in sight at this indoor skydiving centre. (p119)

Wave House Surf serious waves without ever leaving the pool on Sentosa. (p120)

MegaZip Zip-line and rope climb like a sweaty superhero, also on Sentosa. (p121)

GX-5 Extreme Swing A squeal-inducing mega

swing over the Singapore River in Clarke Quay. (p35)

Pinnacle@Duxton Affordable, family-friendly skypark with breathtaking city views and space to run around. (p74)

Outdoor Adventures

Gardens by the Bay Space-age bio-domes, crazy Supertrees, bird's-eye Skyway and a 1-hectare Children's Garden, complete with motion-sensor wet play zones. (p26)

Southern Ridges Complete with dedicated children's playground, a tree-top walk and the occasional monkey sighting. (p142)

Pulau Ubin Hop on a bike and cycle through forest and past colourful shacks on this tranquil, relatively flat, stuck-in-time island. (p90)

Singapore Ducktours Embarrassingly fun tours on a brightly coloured amphibious former military vehicle. (p158)

Best Animal Watching

Singapore Zoo Breakfast with orang-utans at one of the world's

role-model zoological gardens. (p125)

Night Safari Spend the evening with leopards, lions and Himalayan blue sheep at this atmospheric wildlife oasis. (p127)

SEA Aquarium A spectacular, comprehensive aquarium that is one of the world's most impressive. (p119)

Best for a Bite

Rasapura Masters A plethora of food stalls beside an indoor skating rink. (p163)

Casa Verde Family-friendly restaurant in the lush, tropical wonderland of the Botanic Gardens. (p138)

Maxwell Food Centre Cheap, no-fuss street food with a lively, super-casual vibe on the edge of Chinatown. (p75)

Best
Drinking

PHOTO BY WILLIAM CHO/GETTY IMAGES ©

From pink peppercorn Negronis at Tippling Club to Singaporean microbrews at Level 33 and seasonal espresso at Chye Seng Huat Hardware, Singapore has discovered the finer points of drinking. Whatever your poison, you're bound to score: locavore cocktails in a Chinatown basement, craft beers in a hawker centre, or beachside mojitos on Sentosa.

Cut-Price Drinks

Singapore is an expensive city to drink in. A beer at most city bars will set you back between S$10 and S$18, with cocktails commonly ringing in between S$20 and S$30. That said, many bars offer decent happy-hour deals, typically stretching from around 5pm to 8pm, sometimes starting earlier and finishing later. Most deals offer two drinks for the price of one or cheaper 'house pours'. On Wednesday, ladies' night promotions offer cheaper (sometimes free) drinks to women. Those who don't mind plastic tables can always swill S$6 bottles of Tiger at the local hawker centre.

Coffee Evolution

While *kopitiams* (coffeeshops) have been serving *kopi* (local coffee) for generations, Singapore's speciality coffee scene is a more recent phenomenon. Inspired by Australia's artisanal coffee culture, contemporary cafes such as Artistry are brewing seasonal beans, using either espresso machines or 'third wave' brewing techniques such as AeroPress. Also on the increase are cafes sourcing and roasting their own beans, the best of which include Chye Seng Huat Hardware and Nylon Coffee Roasters.

Best Cocktails

Operation Dagger Cutting-edge cocktails in a cognoscenti, underground location. (p78)

Tippling Club Boundary-pushing libations from the bar that raised the bar. (p78)

Spiffy Dapper Bespoke gins and clever surprises from top-tier barkeeps. (p79)

Maison Ikkoku An intimate, upstairs cocktail den in eclectic Kampong Glam. (p107)

Best for Beers

Level 33 Slurp made-on-site beers 33 floors above the city. (p43)

Smith Street Taps A rotating cast of international craft and premium suds in a Chinatown hawker centre. (p79)

Rooftop vistas over Singapore at dusk

Druggists Twenty-three taps pouring in-the-know brews in trendy Jalan Besar. (p107)

RedDot Brewhouse Local microbrews in a tranquil Dempsey setting. (p137)

Best for Wine

Wine Connection Diverse and interesting wines at toast-worthy prices in Robertson Quay. (p43)

Ô Batignolles A snug French bistro pouring affordable wines from independent vineyards. (p80)

Best Heritage Settings

Raffles Hotel Sip a Sling (if only for the novelty value) where Somerset

Maugham once slumbered. (p42)

Colbar Knock back beers at a time-warped colonial mess. (p150)

Green Door Relax alfresco at a converted military barracks in Dempsey. (p136)

Emerald Hill Road Post-shopping drinks on a heritage street off Orchard Rd (p75).

Best for Coffee & Tea

Chye Seng Huat Hardware Superlative espresso, filter coffee, on-site roasting and classes. (p107)

Nylon Coffee Roasters A small, mighty espresso bar and roaster in up-and-coming Everton Park. (p75)

Strangers' Reunion Sucker-punch joe from multi-award-winning barista Ryan Tan. (p80)

Landing Point A posh hotel lounge serving Singapore's finest high tea. (p41)

L'Espresso Another afternoon-tea winner off Orchard Rd. (p57)

Best Clubs

Zouk A multivenue legend with top-tier international DJs on the decks. (p43)

Kyō Japanese-inspired club in a one-time bank in the CBD. (p80)

Best
Entertainment

Singapore's nightlife calendar is generally booked solid. There's live music, theatre and adrenalin-pumping activities year-round, while at certain times of the year the Red Dot explodes into a flurry of car racing, cultural festivals and hot-ticket music events. Then, when it all gets too much, Singapore's spas are waiting in the wings.

RICHARD I'ANSON/GETTY IMAGES ©

Live Music

An enthusiastic local music scene thrives (to a point). Esplanade – Theatres on the Bay hosts regular free performances, and is home to the Singapore Symphony Orchestra. Top-tier international talent is showcased at both the Singapore International Jazz Festival and indie favourite St Jerome's Laneway Festival.

Chinese Opera

Chinese opera, also known by the Malay term *wayang* (performance), includes indoor performances and street opera, the latter usually staged during religious events such as the Hungry Ghost Festival. Although its popularity has decreased over time, groups such as the Chinese Theatre Circle and Kreta Ayer People's Theatre keep the centuries-old tradition alive.

Film

Singaporeans love to watch movies and, at around S$12.50 per ticket, it's great value. Multiplex cinemas abound, with many located in larger malls. Beyond them, the Rex Cinemas runs Bollywood films, while the annual Singapore International Film Festival screens independent and art-house films. Singapore's cinemas are chilly, so wear something warm.

☑ **Top Tip**

▶ Check what's on and buy tickets at www.sistic.com.sg. Expect to pay from S$20 to S$70 for a ticket to a local theatre production, S$100 to S$250 for international music acts, and S$65 to S$200 for big-budget musicals. Gigs by local music acts are often free; some places have a small cover charge.

Best for Live Music

BluJaz Café Consistently good jazz and blues in Kampong Glam. (p109)

Timbrè @ The Substation Local bands and singer-songwriters in the Colonial District. (p44)

Esplanade – Theatres on the Bay by night

Crazy Elephant (Map p30, C3; 📞6337 7859; www.crazyelephant. sg; 01-03/04, 3E River Valley Rd; Ⓜ Clarke Quay) Rock, gutsy blues and a party vibe in tourist-favourite Clarke Quay.

Esplanade – Theatres on the Bay Polished performances spanning classical to rock at a world-famous cultural venue. (p43)

Timbre+ Street art, food trucks and live pop, rock, folk and more Monday to Saturday nights. (p149)

Best for Theatre

Singapore Repertory Theatre A world-class repertoire including seasonal Shakespeare at Fort Canning Park. (p44)

Wild Rice Reinterpreted classics, new works and striking sets. (p110)

Esplanade – Theatres on the Bay Polished productions, from off-Broadway plays to children's theatre. (p43)

TheatreWorks New commissions and international collaborations. (Map p30, A3; 📞6737 7213; www.theatreworks.org.sg; 72-13 Mohamed Sultan Rd)

Toy Factory Productions Bilingual company famed for its provocative works and intercultural collaborations. (p82)

Best for Chinese Opera

Chinese Theatre Circle Chinese opera talks, performances and meals in Chinatown. (p82)

Kreta Ayer People's Theatre Gripping Chinese tales from an independent Chinatown outfit. (p81)

Best for Classic & Indie Films

Screening Room Cult and classic flicks in an intimate suite in Chinatown. (p83)

Rex Cinemas Bollywood hits on the edge of Little India. (p109)

Best Spectator Sports

Formula One Grand Prix (www.singapore-f1-grand-prix. com; September)The F1 night race screams around Marina Bay.

Rugby Sevens (www.singapore7s.sg; April) Part of the World Rugby Cup series.

Singapore Turf Club Join the locals for a hugely popular day out at the races. (p150)

Best
Views & Vistas

Admit it: posting hot travel shots online to torture friends is fun. And while it might surprise you, Singapore makes the perfect partner in crime. From dramatic skyline panoramas to close-up shots of brightly coloured shutters, market produce and lurid tropical flora, the city is ridiculously photogenic. So take aim, shoot and expect no shortage of gratifying Likes.

KIMBERLEY COOLE/GETTY IMAGES ©

Best Skyline Vistas

Smoke and Mirrors Point-blank views of the Marina Bay skyline from the National Gallery Singapore. (p41)

1-Altitude 360-degree island views await at the world's tallest alfresco bar, 282m above CBD traffic. (p43)

Pinnacle@Duxton A panoramic sweep of shophouses, skyscrapers and cargo from atop the world's tallest public housing complex. (p74)

Southbridge A gob-smacking view of ambitious downtown towers, elegant colonial buildings and gliding boats on the Singapore River below. (p41)

Best for Architecture Buffs

Gardens by the Bay High-tech trees, epic bio-domes, a soaring indoor waterfall and striking sculptures. (p26)

National Gallery Singapore A breathtaking synergy of colonial architecture and innovative contemporary design. (p24)

Chinatown Ornate heritage shophouses and smoky temples with stories to tell.

Marina Bay Sands A three-tower sci-fi fantasy. (p34)

Emerald Hill Road An evocative mix of lantern-lit shophouses and elegant, early-20th-century residences. (p52)

Best Is-This-Really Singapore?

Little India Colouring-book facades, shrines and garland stalls, mini mountains of spice and dazzling saris.

Kampong Glam An *Arabian Nights* fantasy of late-night sheesha cafes, intricate Persian rugs and a whimsical, golden-domed mosque.

Pulau Ubin Tin-roof shacks, free-roaming farm animals and rambling jungle wilderness channel a Singapore long since lost.

Geylang Road, Geylang An after-dark demimonde of neon-lit karaoke bars, *kopitiams* and seedy side streets pimped with temples and hookers.

Best
For Free

Believe it or not, it is possible to savour some of Singapore's top offerings without reaching for your wallet. Whether you're into ancient artefacts, contemporary art, million-dollar light shows or live music gigs, you're bound to find it, free of charge. And then there's the simple pleasure of hitting the city's older, colour-saturated neighbourhoods, where daily life is the best show in town.

JOHN ELK III/GETTY IMAGES ©

Best Always-Free Museums

Baba House One of Singapore's best-preserved Peranakan dwellings. (p72)

Changi Museum & Chapel A moving tribute to Singapore's darkest wartime chapter. (p91)

Best Sometimes-Free Museums

National Museum of Singapore Enjoy free entry to the museum's Living Galleries daily from 6pm to 8pm. (p28)

Singapore Art Museum Singapore's main museum of contemporary art is free between 6pm and 9pm on Friday. (p32)

Best Free Art Galleries

NUS Museum Three well-curated galleries showcasing ancient and modern Asian art and artefacts. (p146)

Gillman Barracks Top-tier private galleries from cities like New York and Berlin at a former British military barracks. (p147)

Best Free Entertainment

Esplanade – Theatres on the Bay Singapore's striking arts hub has no shortage of free events, from live-music gigs to art exhibitions and film screenings. (p43)

Marina Bay Sands Home to Wonder Full, a twice-nightly light, laser and water spectacular choreographed to a stirring score. (p34)

Gardens by the Bay Singapore's 21st-century Eden hosts the twice-nightly Garden Rhapsody sound-and-light show. (p26)

Best Free Natural Highs

Singapore Botanic Gardens One of the city-state's greatest attractions, with free tours and seasonal opera to boot. (p130)

Southern Ridges Free forest-canopy strolling, striking architectural features and breathtaking views. (p142)

Best
Museums

Singapore is well endowed with museums, from the tiny and obscure to the ambitious and interactive. You'll find the biggest and the best in the Colonial District, where collections dive into the history, culture and art of Singapore and the continent it belongs to. Beyond them is a kooky booty of unexpected treasures, from reconstructed Chinatown slums to haunting wartime memorials.

SUHAIMI ABDULLAH/GETTY IMAGES ©

Cheaper Admission

Museums in Singapore are usually free to children aged six years and under, and most offer significant discounts to full-time students and seniors; bring photo ID. Concessions aside, some tourist attractions offer combination tickets which can also save you money. Among these are a Singapore Zoo and Night Safari combo. Sentosa Island offers its own set of combination tickets. Called Sentosa Fun Passes (www.sentosa.com.sg/state-specials/sentosa-fun-pass), the tickets cover three, five or 20 island attractions respectively.

Lest They Forget

Singapore's WWII experience was a watershed period in its history. You'll see it covered in depth in many museums, including the National Museum of Singapore and the Changi Museum and Chapel. It's also commemorated at several wartime sites, including a British fort on Sentosa, the battleground of Bukit Chandu (Opium Hill) and a former bunker in Fort Canning Park. Not surprisingly, the trauma of occupation and Singapore's tetchy postwar relations with its larger neighbours have fuelled its obsession with security today.

Best for Art & Handicrafts

National Gallery Singapore Singapore's newest cultural asset showcases 19th- and 20th-century regional art. (p24)

Asian Civilisations Museum A Pan-Asian treasure trove of precious decorative arts, religious artefacts, art and textiles. (p32)

NUS Museum Permanent and temporary exhibitions of Asian ceramics and art. (p146)

Singapore Art Museum Sharp exhibits of contemporary Southeast Asian art. (p32)

Gillman Barracks A rambling artillery of private galleries exhibiting modern and contemporary artists from around the world. (p147)

Display of historical Chinese workers quarters, Asian Civilisations Museum

Best for
Old Singapore

National Museum of Singapore Explore centuries of Singaporean highs and lows, from exiled Sumatran princes to modern independence. (p28)

Chinatown Heritage Centre Relive the gritty, chaotic and overcrowded Chinatown of yesteryear. (p66)

Images of Singapore Live A child-friendly interactive panorama spanning six centuries of local history. (p120)

Best Peranakan
Pickings

Peranakan Museum Delve into the Peranakan world of marriage, storytelling, fashion, feasting and mourning in atmospheric, multimedia galleries. (p32)

Baba House Step into the private world of a wealthy Peranakan family, c 1928, at one of Singapore's most beautiful historic homes. (p72)

Katong Antique House A cluttered collection of historical objects and stories from one of Singapore's leading Peranakan historians. (p87)

Best for War
History

Changi Museum & Chapel Sobering reflections on courage and cruelty during the WWII Japanese occupation. (p91)

Fort Siloso Slip into subterranean tunnels at this ill-fated defence fort on the island of Sentosa. (p120)

Reflections at Bukit Chandu A gripping retelling of the Japanese invasion atop former battlefield Opium Hill. (p143)

Battlebox In Fort Canning Park, this haunting underground complex documents the swift fall of Singapore. (p33)

Best
Escapes

CARLINA TETERIS/GETTY IMAGES ©

Energy meridians feeling blocked? When you have a population density of 7697 people per sq km, it's not surprising. Thankfully, Singapore has myriad ways to revive and refocus weary souls (and soles), from soothing forest canopy walks and island cycling tracks to decadent spa retreats and bargain priced reflexology joints. Whatever your budget, slow, deep breaths are just around the corner.

City of Parks

Singapore's parks are often masterpieces of design and landscaping, from the renowned Botanic Gardens to the forests of the Southern Ridges. A huge network of park connectors enables cyclists and runners to basically circumnavigate the island without ever encountering a road. For network routes, maps and information on events and guided tours (some free), see www.nparks.gov.sg.

The Rubdown

Tight muscles have no shortage of salvation, with midrange to luxe spas in most malls and five-star hotels, and a plethora of cheaper lo-fi joints in less-fashionable malls like People's Park Plaza. The latter is packed with stalls offering reflexology, shiatsu and even pools of fish that happily nibble away your dead skin cells. Rates vary from around S$25 for a foot massage to over S$200 for a full-day package.

Best Green Spaces

Southern Ridges Thick forest and skyline views dot this ribbon of parks and reserves. (p142)

Singapore Botanic Gardens A manicured paradise with a slice of ancient rainforest. (p130)

Pulau Ubin Cycle your worries away on this quaint, once-upon-a-time island. (p90)

Night Safari For a different kind of nightlife. (p127)

Fort Canning Park A historically significant oasis in the heart of the city. (p32)

Best for Pampering

Remède Spa Luxe treatments just off Orchard Rd. (p52)

Spa Esprit Heavenly treatments in green, serene Dempsey Hill. (p134)

People's Park Complex Low-cost reflexology in a throwback mall in hyperactive Chinatown. (p74)

Survival Guide

Survival Guide

Before You Go

When to Go

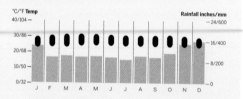

°C/°F Temp
40/104 —

30/86 —
20/68 —
10/50 —
0/32 —

Rainfall inches/mm
— 24/600

16/400

8/200

0

J F M A M J J A S O N D

➡ Singapore is tropical and humid year-round.

➡ School holidays fall in June and July, the hottest time, so try to avoid travelling in these months if possible.

Book Your Stay

☑ **Top Tip** In Singapore's midrange and top-end hotels, room rates are about supply and demand, fluctuating daily. Travellers planning a trip to Singapore need to keep this in mind, especially if you're planning to come here during a major event. For example, room prices triple during the Formula One night race.

Useful Websites

➡ **Lonely Planet** (lonelyplanet.com/singapore) Destination information, hotel bookings, traveller forum and more.

➡ **Your Singapore** (www.yoursingapore.com) Official tourism board website.

➡ **Honeycombers** (www.thehoneycombers.com) A good online guide to Singapore, covering events, eating, drinking and shopping.

➡ **City Nomads** (www.citynomads.com) A handy website with reviews and event listings.

➡ **Sistic** (www.sistic.com.sg) One-stop shop for tickets to concerts and shows in Singapore. Useful events calendar too.

Best Budget

➡ **Adler** (www.adlerhostel.com) This self-proclaimed 'postel' comes with Chinese antiques just near the Chinatown MRT.

➡ **Bunc@Radius** (www.bunchostel.com) Delivers cheap chic in the backpacker heartland of Little India.

➡ **5Footway.Inn Project Boat Quay** (www.5footwayinn.com) A new-school hostel with cal art and a killer location right on Boat Quay.

Best Midrange

➡ **Wanderlust** (www.wanderlusthotel.com) Idiosyncratic rooms packed with imagination, quirkiness and designer twists in intriguing Little India.

➡ **Lloyd's Inn** (www.lloydinn.com) Minimalist boutique hotel a short stroll from Orchard Rd.

➡ **Holiday Inn Express Clarke Quay** (www.hiexpress.com) A fresh, good-value option close to the Quays and Chinatown.

Best Top End

➡ **Fullerton Bay Hotel** (www.fullertonbayhotel.com) Elegant, light-filled luxury perched right on Marina Bay.

➡ **Parkroyal on Pickering** (www.parkroyalhotels.com) A striking architectural statement, with hanging gardens and a stunning infinity pool.

➡ **Capella Singapore** (www.capellahotels.com/singapore) Cascading pools, lush jungle gardens and svelte, chic interiors on Sentosa.

➡ **Park Regis** (www.parkregissingapore.com) Attentive service, modern rooms

and a fantastic pool just a stone's throw from Chinatown and the Quays.

Arriving in Singapore

From Changi Airport

This international **airport** (Map p90; ☎ 6595 6868; www.changiairport.com; Airport Blvd; 🛜; Ⓜ Changi Airport) is 20km northeast of Singapore Central Business District (CBD), has three main terminals, with a fourth terminal scheduled to open in 2017.

➡ **Bus** Public bus 36 runs from Terminals 1, 2 and 3 to Orchard Rd and the Colonial District (S$1.85, one hour). Buses leave roughly every five to 15 minutes, the first departing just after 6am and the last just before 11pm.

➡ **Airport shuttle** Faster and more convenient are the airport shuttle buses (adult S$9, children S$6) which run every 15 to 30 minutes, 24 hours a day, and drop passengers

at any hotel, except for those on Sentosa and in Changi Village. Shuttle buses leave from Terminals 1, 2 and 3. Go to the Ground Transport Desk in the arrival halls.

➡ **MRT** Trains run into town from the airport from 5.30am to midnight; public buses run from 6am to midnight. Both the train and bus trip cost from S$1.85.

➡ **Taxi** A taxi into the city will cost anywhere from S$20 to S$40, and up to 50% more between midnight and 6am, plus airport surcharges.

Train

Malaysian company Keretapi Tanah Melayu Berhad (www.ktmb.com.my) runs trains from Kuala Lumpur to JB Sentral station in Johor Bahru. From here, a shuttle train runs across the strait to **Woodlands Train Checkpoint** (11 Woodlands Crossing; 🚌 170, Causeway Link Express from Queen St terminal) in Singapore. Tickets for the shuttle (S$5) can be bought at the JB Sentral counter.

Bus

➜ Numerous private companies run comfortable bus services to Singapore from many destinations in Malaysia, including Melaka and Kuala Lumpur, as well as from destinations such as Hat Yai in Thailand. Many of these services terminate at **Golden Mile Complex** (☏6291 6945; www.estate. sg/golden-mile-complex; 5001 Beach Rd; dishes from S$3.50; ◷10am-10pm, some eateries 24hr; Ⓜ Lavender, Nicoll Hwy), close to Kampong Glam. You can book online at www.busonlineticket.com.

➜ From Johor Bahru in Malaysia, **Causeway Link** (www.causewaylink. com.my) commuter buses run regularly to various locations in Singapore (one way S$3.30, every 15 to 30 minutes, roughly 6am to 11.30pm), including Newton Circus, Jurong East Bus Terminal and Kranji MRT station.

Boat

Ferry services from Malaysia and Indonesia arrive at various ferry terminals in Singapore.

Changi Point Ferry Terminal (☏6542 7944; 51 Lorong Bekukong; ◷24hr; Ⓜ Tanah Merah, then bus 2)

HarbourFront Cruise & Ferry Terminal (Map p144; G5; ☏6513 2200; www.singaporecruise.com; 1 Maritime Sq; Ⓜ HarbourFront)

Tanah Merah Ferry Terminal (☏6513 2200; www. singaporecruise.com; 50 Tanah Merah Ferry Rd; Ⓜ Tanah Merah, then bus 35M)

Getting Around

☑ The smartphone app 'gothere.sg' will guide you from your location to your destination via different public transport options; it also provides an approximate taxi fare guide.

Mass Rapid Transit (MRT)

➜ The Mass Rapid Transit (MRT) subway system is the easiest, quickest and most comfortable way to get around Singapore. The system operates from 5.30am to midnight, with trains at peak times running every two to three minutes, and off-peak every five to seven minutes.

➜ The system consists of five colour-coded lines: North–South (red), North–East (purple), East–West (green), Circle Line (yellow) and Downtown (blue). An extension of the Downtown line – known as Downtown 3 – is scheduled to open in 2017.

➜ Single-trip tickets cost from S$1.40 to S$2.50 (plus a 10c refundable deposit), but if you're using the MRT a lot it can become a hassle buying and refunding tickets for every journey. A lot more convenient is the EZ-link card.

Bus

➜ Singapore's extensive bus service is clean, efficient and regular, reaching every corner of the island. The two main operators are **SBS Transit** (☏1800 287 2727; www.sbstransit.com.sg) and **SMRT** (☏1800 336 8900; www.smrt.com.sg). Both offer similar services.

➜ Bus fares range from S$1 to S$2.10 (less with an EZ-link card). When you board the bus, drop the exact money into the fare box (no change s given), or tap your EZ-link card or Singapore Tourist Pass on the reader as you board, then again when you get off.

➜ Train operator SMRT also runs late-night bus services between the city and various suburbs from 11.30pm to 2.30am on Fridays, Saturdays and the eve of public holidays. The flat rate per journey is S$4.50. See the website for route details.

Taxi

➜ You can flag down a taxi any time, but in the city centre taxis are technically not allowed to stop anywhere except at designated taxi stands.

➜ Finding a taxi in the city at certain times is harder than it should be. These include during peak hours, at night or when it's raining. Many cab drivers change shifts between 4pm and 5pm, making it notoriously difficult to score a taxi then.

➜ The fare system is also complicated, but thankfully it's all metered, so there's no haggling over fares. The basic flagfall

is S$3 to S$3.40 then S$0.22 for every 400m.

➜ There's a whole raft of surcharges to note, among them 50% of the metered fare from midnight to 6am and 25% of the metered fare between 6am and 9.30am Monday to Friday and from 6pm to midnight daily. Airport journeys incur a surcharge of S$5 from 5pm to midnight Friday to Sunday and S$3 at all other times. Telephone bookings incur a surcharge of S$2.30 to S$8.

➜ Payment by credit card incurs a 10% surcharge. You can also pay using

your EZ-link transport card. For a comprehensive list of fares and surcharges, visit www.taxisingapore.com.

Comfort Taxi and CityCab (☏ 6552 1111)

Premier Taxis (☏ 6363 6888)

SMRT Taxis (☏ 6555 8888)

Travel Passes

There are two kinds of pass for Singapore public transport that save a lot of hassle buying tickets every time you travel.

➜ Buy the **EZ-link card** (www.ezlink.com.sg) from the customer service counters at MRT stations for S$12 (which includes a S$5 nonrefundable deposit). The card can also be bought at 7-Elevens for S$10 (which also includes a S$5 nonrefundable deposit). The card is valid on all MRT and bus services and can be topped up with cash or by ATM cards at station ticket machines.

➜ The **Singapore Tourist Pass** (www.thesingaporetouristpass.com.sg) offers unlimited train and bus travel for S$10 (plus a S$10 refundable deposit). The pass is valid for one day.

Essential Information

....

Customs

→ You are not allowed to bring tobacco into Singapore unless you pay duty. You will be slapped with a hefty fine if you fail to declare and pay.

→ You are permitted 1L each of wine, beer and spirits duty free. Alternatively, you are allowed 2L of wine and 1L of beer, or 2L of beer and 1L of wine. You need to have been out of Singapore for more than 48 hours and to anywhere but Malaysia.

→ It's illegal to bring chewing gum, firecrackers, obscene or seditious material, gun-shaped cigarette lighters, endangered species or their by-products and pirated recordings or publications with you.

Discounts

→ If you arrived on a Singapore Airlines or Silk Air flight, you can get discounts at shops, restaurants and attractions by presenting your boarding pass. See www.singaporeair.com/boardingpass for information.

Electricity

→ Plugs are of the three-pronged, square-pin type. Electricity runs at 230V and 50Hz cycles.

230V/50Hz

Emergencies

→ **Ambulance and Fire** ☎995

→ **Police** ☎999

Holidays

New Year's Day 1 January

Chinese New Year Three days in January/February

Good Friday April

Labour Day 1 May

Vesak Day June

Hari Raya Puasa July

National Day 9 August

Hari Raya Haji September

Deepavali November

Christmas Day 25 December

Money

→ The country's unit of currency is the Singapore dollar (S$), locally referred to as the 'singdollar', which is made up of 100 cents.

→ Singapore uses 5¢, 10¢, 20¢, 50¢ and S$1 coins, while notes come in denominations of S$2, S$5, S$10, S$50, S$100, S$500 and S$1000.

→ ATMs and moneychangers are widely available.

→ Credit cards are accepted in most shops and restaurants.

Business Hours

Opening hours can vary between individual businesses. General opening hours are as follows.

Banks 9.30am-4.30pm Monday to Friday; some branches open 10am-6pm or later. 9.30am-noon or later Saturday.

Restaurants noon-2pm and 6-10pm. Casual restaurants and food courts are open all day.

x

Shops 10am-6pm; some open at 11am. Larger shops and department stores usually close at 9.30pm or 10pm.

Telephone

➡ Singapore's country code is ☎65.

➡ There are no area codes within Singapore; telephone numbers are eight digits unless you are calling toll-free (☎1800).

➡ You can make local and international calls in public phone booths. Most phone booths take phonecards.

➡ Singapore also has credit-card phones that can be used by running your card through the slot.

➡ You can buy a local SIM card for around S$18 (including credit) from post offices, convenience stores and local telco stores – by law you must show your passport to get one. Local carries include **M1** (https://www.m1.com.sg), **SingTel** (http://info.singtel.com) and **StarHub** (www.starhub.com).

Tourist Information

➡ Before your trip, a good place to check for infor-

mation is the website of the **Singapore Tourism Board** (www.yoursingapore.com).

➡ In Singapore, the main branch of **Singapore Visitors Centre @ Orchard** (Map p50; ☎1800 736 2000; www.yoursingapore.com; 216 Orchard Rd; ⊙9.30am-10.30pm; ☎; ⱮSomerset) is filled with knowledgeable staff who can help you organise tours, buy tickets and book hotels. There is free wi-fi, designer souvenirs for sale and a gallery space upstairs, usually with a free exhibition. There is another large branch in **Chinatown** (Map p70; 2 Banda St; ⊙9am-9pm Mon-Fri, to 10pm Sat & Sun; ☎; ⱮChinatown), and a small outlet in **ION Orchard Mall** (☎1800 736 2000; www.yoursingapore.com; Level 1 Concierge, ION Orchard, 2 Orchard Turn; ⊙10am-10pm; ☎; ⱮOrchard), on Orchard Rd.

Travellers with Disabilities

➡ A large government campaign has seen ramps, lifts and other facilities progressively installed around the island. Footpaths in the city are nearly all immaculate, MRT stations all have

lifts and there are some buses and taxis equipped with wheelchair-friendly equipment.

➡ **The Disabled People's Association Singapore** (www.dpa.org.sg) can provide information on accessibility in Singapore.

➡ Download Lonely Planet's free Accessible Travel guide from http://lptravel.to/Accessible-Travel.

Visas

➡ Citizens of most countries are granted 30- or 90-day entry on arrival depending on the country. Citizens of India, Myanmar, the Commonwealth of Independent States and most Middle Eastern countries must obtain a visa before arriving in Singapore. Visa extensions can be applied for at the **Immigration & Checkpoints Authority** (☎6391 6100; www.ica.gov.sg; Level 4, ICA Bldg, 10 Kallang Rd; ⊙8am-4.30pm Mon-Fri, 8am-12.30pm Sat; ⱮLavender).

Language

The official languages of Singapore are Malay, Mandarin, Tamil and English. Malay is the national language, adopted when Singapore was part of Malaysia, but its use is mostly restricted to the Malay community.

The government's long-standing campaign to promote Mandarin, the main nondialectal Chinese language, has been very successful and increasing numbers of Singaporean Chinese now speak it at home. In this chapter we've provided Pinyin (the official system of writing Mandarin in the Roman alphabet) alongside the Mandarin script.

Tamil is the main Indian language in Singapore; others include Malayalam and Hindi. If you read our pronunciation guides for the Tamil phrases in this chapter as if they were English, you'll be understood. The stressed syllables are indicated with italics.

English is widespread and has been the official first language of instruction in schools since 1987. Travellers will have no trouble getting by with only English in Singapore.

To enhance your trip with a phrasebook, visit **lonelyplanet.com**.

Malay

Hello.	Helo.
Goodbye. (when leaving/staying)	Selamat tinggal./ Selamat jalan.
How are you?	Apa khabar?
Fine, thanks.	Khabar baik.
Please. (when asking/offering)	Tolong./ Silakan.
Thank you.	Terima kasih.
Excuse me.	Maaf.
Sorry.	Minta maaf.
Yes./No.	Ya./Tidak.
What's your name?	Siapa nama kamu?
My name is ...	Nama saya ...
Do you speak English?	Bolehkah anda berbicara Bahasa Inggeris?
I don't understand.	Saya tidak faham.
How much is it?	Berapa harganya?
Can I see the menu?	Minta senarai makanan?
Please bring the bill.	Tolong bawa bil.
Where are the toilets?	Tandas di mana?
Help!	Tolong!

Mandarin

Hello./Goodbye.	你好。/再见。	Nǐhǎo./Zàijiàn.
How are you?	你好吗?	Nǐhǎo ma?
Fine. And you?	好。你呢?	Hǎo. Nǐ ne?
Please ...	请……	Qǐng ...
Thank you.	谢谢你。	Xièxie nǐ.

Excuse me. (to get attention)

劳驾。   Láojià.

Excuse me. (to get past)

借光。   Jièguāng.

Sorry.

对不起。   Duìbùqǐ.

Yes./No.

是。/不是。   Shì./Bùshì.

What's your name?

你叫什么   Nǐ jiào shénme

名字？   míngzi?

My name is ...

我叫……   Wǒ jiào ...

Do you speak English?

你会说   Nǐ huìshuō

英文吗？   Yīngwén ma?

I don't understand.

我不明白。   Wǒ bù míngbái.

How much is it?

多少钱？   Duōshǎo qián?

Can I see the menu?

能不能给我看   Néng bù néng gěiwǒ

一下菜单？   kàngyīxià càidān?

Please bring the bill.

请给我账单。   Qǐng gěiwǒ zhàngdàn.

Where are the toilets?

厕所在哪儿？   Cèsuǒ zài nǎr?

Help!

救命！   Jiùmìng!

Tamil

Hello.

வணக்கம்.   va·*nak*·kam

Goodbye.

போய வருகிறேன்.   *po*·i va·*ru*·ki·reyn

How are you?

நீங்கள் நலமா?   *neeng*·kal na·*la*·maa

Fine, thanks. And you?

நலம், நன்றி.   na·*lam* nan·dri

நீங்கள்?   *neeng*·kal

Please.

தயவு செய்து.   ta·ya·*vu* chey·*tu*

Thank you.

நன்றி.   nan·dri

Excuse me.

தயவு செய்து.   ta·ya·*vu* sei·*du*

Sorry.

மன்னிக்கவும்.   man·*nik*·ka·vum

Yes./No.

ஆமாம். / இல்லை.   aa·maam/*il*·lai

What's your name?

உங்கள் பெயர்   ung·kal pe·*yar*

என்ன?   en·na

My name is ...

என் பெயர்...   en pe·*yar* ...

Do you speak English?

நீங்கள் ஆங்கிலம்   *neeng*·kal *aang*·ki·lam

பேசுவீர்களா?   pey·chu·*veer*·ka·la

I don't understand.

எனக்கு   e·*nak*·ku

விளங்கவில்லை.   vi·*lang*·ka·vil·*lai*

How much is it?

இது என்ன   i·*tu* en·na

விலை?   vi·*lai*

I'd like the bill/menu, please.

எனக்கு தயவு   e·*nak*·ku ta·ya·*vu*

செய்து   chey·*tu*

விலைச்சீட்டு/   vi·*laich*·cheet·tu/

உணவுப்பட்டியல்   u·na·*vup*·pat·ti·yal

கொடுங்கள்.   ko·*tung*·kal

Where are the toilets?

கழிவறைகள்   ka·*zi*·va·rai·kal

எங்கே?   *eng*·key

Help!

உதவு!   u·ta·*vi*

Behind the Scenes

Send Us Your Feedback

We love to hear from travellers – your comments help make our books better. We read every word, and we guarantee that your feedback goes straight to the authors. Visit **lonelyplanet.com/contact** to submit your updates and suggestions.

Note: We may edit, reproduce and incorporate your comments in Lonely Planet products such as guidebooks, websites and digital products, so let us know if you don't want your comments reproduced or your name acknowledged. For a copy of our privacy policy visit lonelyplanet.com/privacy.

Ria de Jong's Thanks

Thank you to my destination editor Sarah Reid for holding my hand through my Lonely Planet adventure, and to Cristian Bonetto who trod the path before me. To my parents and sister who nurtured my love of the road less travelled, to my travelling circus tribe Craig, Cisca and William, and to Jen, who keeps us all in line.

Cristian Bonetto's Thanks

Sincere thanks to Helen Burge, Honey Lee, Carolyn Ng, Sharon Vu, Myra Tan, Michelle Chua and Richie Raupe.

Acknowledgements

Cover photograph: Gardens by the Bay, Marina Bay
Maurizio Rellini/4Corners ©

This Book

This 5th edition of Lonely Planet's *Pocket Singapore* guidebook was researched and written by Ria de Jong and curated by Cristian Bonetto. The previous two editions were written by Cristian Bonetto. This guidebook was produced by the following:

Destination Editor
Sarah Reid

Product Editors
Jessica Ryan, Catherine Naghten

Senior Cartographer
Julie Sheridan

Book Designer
Gwen Cotter

Assisting Editors Sarah Bailey, Kate Morgan, Anne Mulvaney, Lauren O'Connell, Kristin Odijk.

Cover Researcher
Naomi Parker

Thanks to Jennifer Carey, Sandie Kestell, Anne Mason, Mazzy Prinsep, Angela Tinson, Dora Whitaker.

Index

See also separate subindexes for:

Eating p189

Drinking p190

Entertainment p191

Shopping p191

Sights 000
Map Pages **000**

🍴 Eating

Our Writers

Ria de Jong

Writer Ria started life in Asia, born in Sri Lanka to Dutch/Australian parents; she has always relished the hustle and excitement of this continent of contrasts. After growing up in Townsville, Australia, Ria moved to Sydney as a features writer before packing her bags for a five-year stint in the Philippines. Moving to Singapore in 2015 with her husband and two small children, Ria is loving discovering every nook and cranny of this tiny city, country, nation. This is Ria's second Singapore update for Lonely Planet. Follow Ria on Twitter @ria_in_transit.

Cristian Bonetto

Curator Cristian has contributed to over 30 Lonely Planet guides to date, including *New York City*, *Italy*, *Venice & the Veneto*, *Naples & the Amalfi Coast*, *Denmark*, *Copenhagen*, *Sweden* and *Singapore*. His musings on travel, food, culture and design appear in numerous publications around the world, including the *Telegraph* (UK) and *Corriere del Mezzogiorno* (Italy). When not on the road, you'll find the reformed playwright and TV scriptwriter in his beloved hometown, Melbourne. Follow Cristian on Twitter @cristianbonetto.

Published by Lonely Planet Global Limited
CRN 554153
5th edition – June 2017
ISBN 978 1 7865 7532 6
© Lonely Planet 2017   Photographs © as indicated 2017
10 9 8 7 6 5 4 3 2 1
Printed in Malaysia